Polemicization

Taking on the Political
Series Editors: Benjamin Arditi and Jeremy Valentine
International Advisory Editors: Jane Bennet, Michael Dillon
and Michael J. Shapiro

Polemicization: The Contingency of the Commonplace
Benjamin Arditi and Jeremy Valentine

Cinematic Political Thought: Narrating Race, Nation and Gender
Michael J. Shapiro

Polemicization

The Contingency of the Commonplace

Benjamin Arditi and Jeremy Valentine

NEW YORK UNIVERSITY PRESS
Washington Square, New York

First published in the U.S.A. in 1999 by
NEW YORK UNIVERSITY PRESS
Washington Square
New York, NY 10003

CIP data available from the Library of Congress
ISBN 0-8147-0688-6 (cloth)
ISBN 0-8147-0689-4 (paperback)

Typeset in 11 on 13 Sabon
by Hewer Text Ltd, Edinburgh, and

Contents

Preface

Polemicization refers to a type of engagement through which the space of polemic is itself transformed. This transformation is not one of the victory of one of the participants over the other – for example, in the form of domination or annihilation – as it extends to the transformation of the participants in the polemic themselves. Polemicization is an aleatory process. It dislocates positions through the process of their enunciation. It is because of this that it is not reducible to the status of a referent or object. This is a large claim and as such could be easily misunderstood, both to support and refute it. As this book is itself polemical there may also appear to be an element of performative contradiction in its very enunciation. We could not possibly prevent reactions and perceptions of this nature. What we can do is lay out the intellectual and empirical forces that have led us to this claim, which is to say, our reactions to and perceptions of the present conjuncture within which it is enunciated. Given the overdetermined and fluid nature of any conjuncture, this could hardly pretend to be exhaustive. Any conjuncture is a work rather than an object given beforehand. Therefore, the description will inevitably betray a degree of partisanship.

Perhaps the quickest way into this is through a hastily improvised and highly impressionistic sociology of knowledge that takes contemporary critical cultural and political debate as its object or field, and which recognizes that this debate is not confined to particular disciplines or institutions. The major organizing themes of this field are identity and difference. There is nothing new or especially innovative about these terms. They are derived from a variety of perspectives across the hard and soft sciences. What is curious about their use in the present conjuncture is the manner in which they tend to be presented as poles of identification, as positions that could be occupied. In this respect they obey one of the most traditional aspirations of Western thought: namely, the desire to condense normative value and empirical existence in a single point. It is as if underlying the circulation of these terms are formulas such as 'one must be open because closure is impossible,' or 'there is difference so be different.' These may contain good advice, yet we are less confident of their logical force. This is for two reasons. Firstly, there is the traditional one: the desire to reconcile value and existence begs the question of why these two terms have ever become distinct, and of how one would know that this is no longer the case. Secondly, there is the contemporary one: the subject who is to act in such a way that the truth of these formulas could be revealed cannot be established, as to do so, or rather to claim to do so, would negate both the values and existence under which such a subject would stand. Polemicization arises from the dynamic of these twin failures; the persistence of antagonism against reconciliation, and the emergence of subjectivation against the stability of a subject. The former takes place through the latter.

In support of this let us consider developments that have occurred around the question of subjectivity and the critique of the subject in the sense of a universal model to which all experience should somehow correspond. Identifying the prevalence of what he calls 'the envy of abjection' across artistic, theoretical and popular cultures, Foster demonstrates that a pervasive desire for victim status arises from the possibility of acquiring the resources that accompany its elevated position. Foster's discussion of 'trauma discourse' is worth citing at length:

> On the one hand, in art and theory, trauma discourse continues the poststructuralist critique of the subject by other means, for again, in a psychoanalytic register, there is no subject of trauma; the position is evacuated, and in this sense the critique of the subject is most radical here. On the other hand, in popular culture, trauma is treated as an event that guarantees the subject, and in this psychologistic register the subject, however disturbed, rushes back as witness, testifier, survivor. Here is indeed a traumatic subject, and it has absolute authority, for one cannot challenge the trauma of another: one can only believe it, even identify with it, or not. *In trauma discourse, then, the subject is evacuated and elevated at once.* And in this way trauma discourse magically resolves two contradictory imperatives in culture today: deconstructive analysis and identity politics. (Foster 1996: 168, original emphasis)

In this context a politics that reads antagonism off of an opposition between the same and the different is redundant; or rather, if a politics occurs through this, it remains at the administrative level in the sense that one is maintained in one's place, and one's place becomes where one wants to be. The abject nature of one's existence simply becomes the mark of its authenticity. Berlant (1997) makes a similar, and we believe accurate, observation of how an identification with difference as the authority of otherness has actually panned out in the social context of the United States as a consequence of its circulation through the so-called 'Culture Wars': 'A nationwide estrangement from an imagined hegemonic centre seems now to dignify every citizen's complaint' (100). Notice what has happened here. The status of the centre and its hegemonic power is imagined. It enjoys the status of a fantasy. There must be a center in order to occupy a position eccentric to it. At the same time difference, the marginal, has acquired the value of trumps in political argument. This means that difference is actually commonplace or hegemonic. It is what one is required to be in order to enjoy the advantages that it provides.

Making this point is not to adopt the position of conservative reaction. No doubt those radical activists that sought to advance the cause of the marginal and unenfranchised never intended such an outcome. Empirically, such groups remain massively disadvantaged in the context of increasing inequalities of wealth and resource access. The point is that the dynamic that originally sustained the contestation of social distribution has become fixed as a position. In other words, difference has become reconciled with the *distribution of appearances* as its organizing logic. This stems from a structural ambiguity in the political value of difference itself. Is the differential status of a social position something to be resisted in so far as it licenses exclusion, or is it something to be celebrated as a mark of alterity, and thus exclusivity? The political logic of difference depends on precisely this duck-rabbit aspect of the term. On occasion it enjoys a somewhat comical aspect, as, for example, when, as a legitimation of exclusion, the underclass is described in terms of the characteristics of low intelligence, lack of motivation, a preference for instant gratification without responsibility and an inability to sustain conventional sexual and social discipline. The problem with this description is that it applies to more or less everyone.

Rancière – whose work we will return to repeatedly – makes the point that the assumption of a plurality of differential identities is the contemporary form of universality (1995a: 177). The inference he draws from this is pessimistic, as it prevents the politicization of universality itself. In other words, in acquiring a universal status difference is simply taken for granted. It is a matter of policing. This is why Rancière insists on the distinction between subjectification and identification, in that the former introduces a new position into a social space, whereas the latter simply reinforces the stability of this space (1998: 37). Subjectification, which is not the same thing as subjectivity, is the production of a new capacity for enunciation that is not a pole of identification. It has no place within the organization of places. It is expressive and disruptive. Identity, on the other hand, simply confirms 'the fact of each person's being in their place, going about their own business there, and having the opinion identical to the fact of being in that place and doing only what there is to do there' (106); that is, one confines oneself to an *ethos*. Consequently, the right to be different becomes the right to be in one's place. In 'trauma discourse' this can only be confirmed by the performance of trauma, the ultimate guarantee of subjectivity beyond dispute.

We can deepen the implications of this. Whereas formerly the purpose of an emphasis on alterity was to undermine the certainty of the same and self-identity, although perhaps only in so far as these were associated with domination, the current situation is somewhat reversed. The discovery of the pervasiveness of alterity has in effect weakened the distinction between the same and the other. In other words, if the dimension of sameness can no longer be reliably located, then neither can that of the other. To use Freud's vocabulary, *Verfremdung*, alienation by means of the other, has been replaced by *Entfremdung*, the condition in which there is no other any more (Baudrillard 1997: 48). This does not mean that we have suddenly entered the transparency of a universal equivalence. Alterity has simply become an object of political calculation. As Critchley asks in his devastating critique of Levinasian sentimentality, to which he opposes Blanchot's account of the other as the horror of neutrality, why should goodness be predicated of alterity (1997: 81)? If goodness cannot be presumed, neither can badness. It is only the weight of a normalizing investment in alterity, even when the other is presented as self-consciously 'bad', that preserves its connotation of goodness. The role of this alterity by default has been correctly diagnosed by Rancière in his account of the 'saturation of consensus' and the 'new social contract' that enforces it. Alterity gives back 'to each person excluded the identity of a mobilized capability and responsibility' in order to 'establish in every derelict dwelling a cell of collective responsibility' (1998: 117). The target of this observation is the substitution of ethics for politics and its reliance on 'the absolute Other to atone for the flaws in the notion of the Same' (135).

In referencing these types of argument we are not seeking to dismiss the pertinence of such notions as sameness or difference, but simply trying to point out that the political dimension of these notions is in inverse proportion to their commonplace nature, to their value as a political or moral currency. A central force in the sedimentation of these terms is the assumption that they can be directly transposed on to a relation between an inside and an outside, a relation that even acquires an epistemological ground in the principle of incommensurability. Again, we can improvise another formula to capture the force of this principle: 'You cannot know me, therefore you must not know me'. Against this our concern is with the political dimension of non-identity or non-belonging that dislocates the identity of the same and the different, an inside and an outside. In many respects this derives from the analysis of *deconstruction*, a name that lacks all propriety. Schematically, this concerns the moment in which thought encounters a limit of some kind in the very attempt to constitute a limit, and thus fails to close in on itself and betrays its own responsibility for the effects of a closure that is posited but never finally achieved. It will always remain an open or undecidable question whether such a limit is established or imposed. Deconstruction, however does not entail anything like a rejection of the validity of this enterprise, as through it deconstruction happens. That said, we are not engaging in yet another argument that proposes that deconstruction should be linked with politics. In our opinion, the link is already there and in this sense we take deconstruction for granted in that we aim to deepen its presence. At the same time, we are also mindful of the way that deconstruction is taken for granted in practice – for example, through its reduction to something like a method of analysis or explanation, or a verb or adjective. In not dwelling on deconstruction we simply seek to establish some distance from its reduction to a commonplace or popular position.[1]

What is clear from deconstruction is that customary approaches to political thought are no longer as satisfactory as they once were. In other words, it is political thinking that we do not take for granted. Indeed, we are concerned with the question as to whether it occurs at all. The central topics and themes around which political thought has hitherto been organized, such as authority, obligation, decision, representation and the like, are best seen as improvised solutions from which a semblance of necessity is produced and not as expressions of predetermined laws or logical conditions. Deconstruction is not a means for rejecting these solutions but for reactivating the questions and problems from which they arise and through which deconstruction takes place. Laclau has given this aspect of deconstruction a somewhat positive expression that identifies the stakes of thinking politically:

> A history of the presence of the political moment in the representation of communitarian spaces in Western thought must therefore be a history of the ways in which incompletion – or dislocation, which amounts to the same thing – has been given a discursive presence. This history could be conceived as an account of the long process by which the community has come to terms with its political nature. (1990: 72)

We do not know if this process is at an end, or even if it has begun. Certainly we would reserve judgement on the issue of a community's capacity to come to terms with its non-identity. To put a slightly different emphasis on this formula, our concern with polemicization is a concern with the production of incompletion or dislocation, the failure of the representation of community and which, as deconstruction, takes place in the very production of such a representation. Such a production does not issue from a centre, even if it seeks to establish one, but attempts a centring, an authoritative distribution of appearances. This means that the contestation of the representation remains within the representation itself as that which falsifies it. In Rancière's terms, this moment of contestation, or what we are calling polemicization, is 'the part that has no part'.[2]

The aim of this book is to deepen the contours of polemicization. In the first chapter we introduce the scope of polemicization by establishing its relation to subjectification. We discuss how political thinking is limited in its attempt to think the antagonistic dimension of subjectification by virtue of the assumption of the ontotheological nature of the political itself. In particular, through an engagement with the work of Claude Lefort, we show how, in the attempt to free itself of ontotheology, the modern notion of the political reproduces it in an 'empty' form. This has critical consequences for how the relation between power and democracy is to be understood.

What limits political thinking is the inherited form of the relation between philosophy and politics, and in particular the assumption of a coincidence between these two terms. In the second chapter we interrogate this relationship by focusing on the way that polemic has been thought as an object of political philosophy itself. In Schmitt we show that the essentially polemical nature of political discourse prevents the constitution of a concept of the political that would comprehend the relation between an outside and an inside as one of antagonism. This relocates the political within the inside, or in Schmitt's terms, the domain of the friend, as that which brings the objectivity of this domain into question. We deepen this account of antagonism by reactivating the critical moment in Kant's philosophical enterprise in order to demonstrate that for Kant this was a means of polemicizing political order and of destabilizing its referential status. We apply this aspect of Kant to a thinker who has acquired the reputation of Kant's contemporary representative: John Rawls. Rawls's work is marked by the absence of any critical impulse. As such it assumes the referential objectivity of political order, and in so doing renders the scope of application of its argument redundant. Against Rawls's assumption that pluralism coincides with itself, and against his belief that this does not involve a metaphysical dimension, we develop an account of the non-identity of plurality derived from Connolly's notion of *pluralization*.

The notion of a plurality that does not correspond to itself poses the issue of the nature of the political subject. In the third chapter we consider how this can be thought. Using Foucault's account of the relation between the subject and power, and connecting this to the radical contingency of modernity, we critically engage with Laclau and Mouffe's account of the discursive constitution of the subject. The argument hinges on the precise location of antagonism. In Laclau and Mouffe this falls between an account of the subject in the construction of hegemony, and an account of the subject as an antagonistic force that destabilizes hegemony by preventing the objectivity of the social. This issues in the distinction between a popular and a democratic subject, the stakes of which are clarified by a discussion of the critical reception Laclau and Mouffe's account of the subject has provoked. On this basis we consider a third option in Laclau and Mouffe's thought. This is the mythical subject, the advantage of which is supposed to lie in its recognition of the plural and decentred experience of subjectivity that accompanies late modernity, or globalized complexity. For us this reinscribes the popular hegemonic subject in mythical form as subject that exists through mourning or nostalgia for a centre. We argue that in this scene antagonism takes the form of the polemicization of its distribution, or the collapse of the distribution of appearances in which it would correspond to itself.

Every difference none the less aspires to such distribution of appearances. Its most recent incarnation is authenticity in one's abjection, which results in what Berlant depicts as a claim to the dignity of every citizen's complaint. A possible underside of this position is that polemics is replaced by increasingly rigid moral codes whereby one renounces the judgement of others in the name of the dignity of every difference. In the end this simply radicalizes the liberal claim to neutrality toward the good. It also lends credibility to a curious resurrection of apartheid, only this time vindicated as a progressive cacophony of self-righteous particular groups. In the final chapter we review some of the inconsistencies in this position, especially with regard to the silent remainder of the question of universality and commonality. Emphatically, this does not aim to reintroduce an ethics of undistorted communication, and even less to assume a shared rationality or a search for consensus. Neither do we reduce the question to the alternative between deliberation and confrontation. Instead we explore a way of thinking universality as a 'measure of incommensurables' arising in scenarios of dispute that also shape the space of polemic among contestants. Here we appeal to Derrida's reflection about undecidability, the challenge of producing singular judgements while at the same time contemplating the generality of the rule. Dispute is the occasion of this challenge, as we will see in the case of rules and generally of whatever passes for a referent. We also appeal again to Rancière, who sees the truth of a universal as a *topos*, the effect of an argumentative plot where the parties hear one another without agreeing with one another: in a word, where polemic is in the order of the day.

Finally, we would like to acknowledge that this work itself arises from a series of polemical engagements. It is only through these that anything has been done. We would specifically like to thank our friends Mick Dillon from Lancaster University and Torben Bech Dyrberg from Roskilde University in Denmark. In a way *Polemicization* was shaped by our community of polemics. Above all, we would like to thank Jackie Jones and especially Nicola Carr, our editor at Edinburgh University Press, who was kind enough to be less polemical than she ought to have been when we were less able than we should have been. Some of the ideas discussed in Chapter 4 were previously published in *Philosophy and Social Criticism*, Vol. 23, No. 3, 1997.

Lancaster and Mexico City
January 1999

Notes

1. The historian Jon Wiener has recently done the job of describing the popular circulation of the word 'deconstruction'. A database survey of newspapers and popular magazines revealed that over a two-year period the word and variants of it appeared in almost 7,000 articles. These included *Reader's Digest*, *TV Guide*, *Entertainment Weekly*, *The New York Times*, *The American Banker*, *Playboy* and *Sports Illustrated*. The television presenter Dan Rather is quoted as proclaiming that 1996 would be 'a pivotal presidential election' because 'this is the first time that we are facing the possibility of deconstruction.' *Forbes* discussed 'The Deconstruction of the Semiconductor Industry' with its readers, and *The New York Times*, in which the word appeared 309 times over two years, declared that *The Perfect Recipe Baking Book* 'deconstructs 50 classic pies, cakes and cookies with paternal and meticulous detail'. See 'Deconstruction Goes Pop', *The Nation*, 7 April 1997. We are grateful to David Oppedissano for this article.
2. This formula has very close resemblances with Honig's notion of 'the remainder' (Honig 1993).

Chapter 1

Polemic and Polemicization

1.1 Polemic and the Commonplace

Polemic is usually understood as a relation between opponents in which a confrontation occurs through the medium of argumentation. This relation relies on various degrees of recognition and exchange between the parties to the dispute in the peculiar sense in that these elements are both its condition and object. The participants are supposed to face each other fully present to themselves and their adversaries. Ideally, the mode of address adopted should confirm this positioning and at the same time represent that which is held in common to be both present as a stake in the dispute and absent as that which is to be settled. Indeed, it is possible to conceive of a dispute in which one of the participants challenges the manner in which he or she is recognized by the other, and may even wish not to be recognized at all. For this to be effective, the disputant remains forced to seek out representations and expressions that would communicate this. This can even include the refusal to communicate, or the avoidance of communication. Equally, the opposite can also be the case. It is possible to conceive of an over-communication wherein an adversary is identified so strongly that no one would correspond to the given representation. In such instances more is revealed about the would-be polemicist than the target of the polemic.

Düttman (1997) gives an excellent example of this through an analysis of the economy of the slogan 'we're queer, we're here, so get fuckin' used to it.' On the surface, this is a demand for recognition addressed to others who do not occupy, or at least do not acknowledge that they occupy, the position of enunciation the phrase describes. The impact of the phrase can be measured in two ways: as a provocation which aims for acceptance within a more inclusive consensus, a puritanical 'political correctness'; and as an ironic affirmation that queer identity does not need to be recognized because it simply exists, like it or not. Both 'demand that one recognize what one no longer needs to recognize' (28). It is a demand to be recognized by the other, the non-queer, *as* something different, as other. The demand is superfluous, merely the expression of a desire for confirmation and institutionalization, and thus dependency in the dialectical sense. The point, however, is that its enunciation destabilizes the ideality of its communication as a face-to-face encounter, or the model of sender → receiver. It is in this dimension that its polemical sense is located, and which 'lies in the equivocation it generates in conflating the "we" of those to whom the demand is addressed and the "we" of those who make it', thus revealing the shifting and impermanent boundaries between 'these subjects, who are not yet subjects' (28).

Naturally, this is contrary to anyone's intention. On the one hand, recognition becomes habitual and domesticated – even if either side of the dispute continues to hate the other virulently. On the other hand, the phrase is uncontrollable, outside the grasp of both those who project it and their targets. Consequently:

> One who demands recognition has already arrived, has already reached the destination still to be attained, and does not require the recognition that is demanded. The polemical presumption here lies in the way in which the one who is to be recognized transforms those who are to bestow recognition into those who require recognition. The roles, the functions, the positions in question thereby find themselves caught up in a constant and uncontrollable process of exchange – in the final analysis it is impossible to decide who should be recognized here and now and who is recognizing whom here and now. (30)

The phrase produces an effect that puts the space of the habitual – the *habitus* – in question. Recognition is suspended, removed from its *telos* through what Düttman calls a tension between the name and anonymity which functions as an '*opening* which makes politics necessary' (32). We would say that through this opening polemic is *polemicized* in the sense that it is not the parties to the dispute that are incommensurable but the scene in which this occurs. This scene does not correspond to itself, which is to say that in these circumstances reliance on instruction and example is no substitute for wit and inventiveness, those improprieties that make for movement. Polemicization is idiomatic.

In this scenario any reliance on a topography of minorities and majorities as the referent of the dispute becomes counterproductive. It simply reduces the incommensurability of the opening to a common measure, and thus eradicates it. Thus, 'a group that identifies itself as a minority can, fundamentally speaking, no longer struggle for recognition and has already become powerless in this struggle' (33).[1] In this instance the self-identification of minorities *as* minorities, or the more likely designation of minorities as that to be identified with as a mode of subjectivation, is perverse. It carries on the work of that which authorizes such an identification in the name of opposition to this very authorization. It grounds the description in a recognition that functions as a verification of that which was thought to be in dispute. This means that the polemic can never occur as such as its terms are sealed against polemicization. It is not surprising that 'minority discourse' often gives rise to some pernicious acts of ventriloquism which render opposition a matter to be administered and the expression of opposition a matter to be policed. They preserve a questionable moral, ethical and material distribution that ensures that each remains domesticated as the majority or minority that each must be.

To polemicize this economy of value we could do much worse than cite Rancière's reactivation of the presence of anonymity, the *proletarii*. This is the Latin word for 'prolific people – people who make children, who merely live and reproduce without a name, without being counted as part of the symbolic order of the city' (1995b: 67). This reactivation can be linked to a further distinction Rancière makes in another dead language between the Greek *ochlos* or turbulent mass, and the *demos*, the people (1995c: 31). This distinction is not one of opposition or contradiction but instead describes the dynamic of a never fully excluded supplement. The significance of the *demos*, the people or the 'we', is that it does not have a unified existence. It is not a subject present to itself across the surface of the social body that it would both inscribe and correspond to (39) but a moment that divides the *ochlos* and prevents it from being constituted as a whole or the unity of a one. It is 'the power to undo all partnerships, gatherings and ordinations' (32). This is because the people is always more or less than itself, always a transformation of the *proletarii/ochlos* in process. It lacks a ground from which it could be derived or to which it could be reduced as an ideal or material referent. 'It is the power of *one more*, the power of *anyone*, which confuses the right ordering of policy' (1995b: 64, original emphasis).[2] The *proletarii* are not one, either as a total unity which subsumes its parts or as an aggregate of entities. In terms of conduct the *demos* is sporadic and inconsistent, a characteristic for which Plato ridiculed democracy, but in which Rancière locates its virtue as 'the art of life in common'. This entails 'a membership in a single world which can only be expressed in adversarial terms, and a coming together which can only occur in conflict' (1995c: 49). The *proletarii* polemicize the *demos*, which is the condition under which one can speak of a *demos* or a people. Otherwise, the people would not be a question that could be posed at all. Belonging would not be at issue and thus the people would not need to be named. The presence of the *proletarii* polemicizes by exceeding the scope of any name.

This relation between the name and anonymity structures political existence. According to Rancière, politics exists:

> First, because there are names which deploy the sphere of appearance of the people, even if in the process such names are apt to become separated from 'things'; second, because the people are always too numerous or too few compared with the form of their manifestation; and third, because the name of the people is at one and the same time the name of the community and the name of a part of – or rather a split in – the community. The gap between people as community and people as division is the site of a fundamental grievance. At the outset, it is not the king but the people who have a double embodiment. (1995c: 96–7)[3]

This doubling of the people arises from an originary division that is itself double. Firstly, within the *demos*, between the *demos* and the *ochlos*, and secondly, between the *eupori*, those who have means, and the *aporoi*, those who do not. This double division is comprehended by the immanence of the *proletarii*, the presence of the horizon of division.[4] The people is different from itself and divided within itself. As such, it is always miscounted and misnamed. On the one hand, everyone is equal to everyone in so far as each is exchangeable with and equivalent to the other, a purely mathematical equality. On the other, some are more equal than others, a geometrical difference.[5] It is the function of government, what Rancière calls the police, to institute and maintain this geometrical difference through which names are assigned and distributed, minorities and majorities are diagrammed. This refers to the sphere of appearance or the mode of visibility of difference. It is the function of politics to contest this. This contestation stems from the impossibility of translating mathematical equality and geometrical difference into a unity of each other that can be named. The name of the *demos* is simply a 'paradoxical measure of incommensurables' and is thus structurally incomplete (1995a: 172). The paradoxical name of this incompletion, which from the point of view of the police represents a lack, but which from the point of view of politics represents an opening, is the *proletarii*. It is that which cannot be assigned to a place derived from the distribution of geometrical proportion. It is not a part of the system of relations between parts which organizes the social order. At the same time it cannot be reduced to a one which could be exchanged or substituted. This is why the *proletarii* is not a thing that can be named or represented but the site of the intersection of two heterogeneous processes in which the geometrical distribution of parts is dislocated by posing the question of mathematical equality,[6] and which does not preexist this encounter but takes place through it. Rancière understands the mode of its enactment in terms of polemic. This site of encounter, or 'the nonplace as place' (1995b: 66), puts into question or polemicizes the name of the community and the names that this organizes, through the double inscription of the *demos*.

This link with the *proletarii*, and thus with the demonstration that the *demos* is not a referent which could be secured through designation, entails that polemic is not a purely theoretical object. Neither is it a completely spontaneous practice. In fact, it postpones this traditional distinction. If this is not normally acknowledged in the prosecution of polemic, it nevertheless remains tacit, retaining all the advantages of 'know-how'. In attempting to define the term one inevitably risks losing that dimension of engagement and confrontation which characterizes it as a shared experience of a peculiar sort. For this reason no one would legislate for polemic, on its behalf as its representative, or elevate it to an end in itself. It is difficult to speak for it and thus to address it directly, and even more so to speak from and within it as a place of enunciation. Above all, it is not an occasion which issues from a decision and takes place within guaranteed parameters. This is because polemicization poses the questions of limits, both of the participants that engage and of the space of engagement where this takes place. Consequently, the notion of a limit or a frontier of some description as the reason for polemic is inadequate, as it is the function of limits that has to be explained.

The problem of the limit can be illustrated by reference to the following remark of Wittgenstein:

> To say 'this combination of words makes no sense' excludes it from the sphere of language and thereby bounds the domain of language. But when one draws a boundary it may be for various kinds of reason. If I surround an area with a fence or a line or otherwise, the purpose may be to prevent

> someone from getting in or out; but it may also be part of a game and the players be supposed, say, to jump over the boundary; or it may show where the property of one man ends and that of another begins; and so on. So if I draw a boundary line that is not yet to say what I am drawing it for. (1983: 138–9)

Not only does a line have to be drawn or made in some fashion, the line itself is radically undecidable. The purpose of the line can only be added as a supplement, a further line that in so far as it is inscribed in the original line thereby undermines its obviousness or purity by revealing the necessity of instruction in its use. Such supplementary inscriptions are interminable, which is why they can only be settled by convention or habit. On reflection this is confirmed by the everyday experience of signs which warn off intruders, of border guards and the like. The wider issue that this raises stems from the effect that this insight has on the principle of incommensurability, or even the assertion of incommensurability as a principle, as the ground of dispute. Incommensurability can only arise through dispute, not as a thing that could be designated or as some reified notion of *alterity*, but as the dislocation of the obviousness of the line that separates the disputants in their togetherness. Incommensurability is something that happens.

This can also be applied to the level of language or the symbolic by reference to Davidson's critique of the scheme/content distinction in his proposition that 'there is no such thing as language.' This is not only because there is no all-encompassing rule with which to decide what the relation is between language and something not language – the 'third dogma of empiricism' – but also because there is no rule to determine when one language ends and another begins. Consequently, this requires that alterity is thought differently from the reified moral sense that the concept has acquired in contemporary critical thought. Alterity is not a thing that can be counterposed to a homogeneous sameness by virtue of a line that is supposed to distinguish them. As Davidson points out:

> It would be equally wrong to announce the glorious news that all mankind – all speakers of language at least – share a common scheme and ontology. For if we cannot intelligibly say that schemes are different, neither can we intelligibly say that they are one. (1984: 198)

Alterity is not a thing or an object that could be identified with or *as*. It is a process. No one, however, could say whether such a process had been completed. This undecidability constitutes the polemicization of the same and the different, and thus of the line supposed to distinguish them.

The impact of this argument can be measured with reference to Laclau's notion of the 'constitutive outside' and its theoretical link with a 'logic of exclusionary limits', which grounds the assertion that 'true limits are always antagonistic' (1994: 169). Here limit is already inscribed with a political value. It is the objectivity of the limit itself. On one side of the limit is located sameness, on the other difference. This is a reciprocal relation of mirrors. In fact, the existence of these two terms depends on the antagonistic relation that unites them such that 'all social order . . . can only affirm itself in so far as it represents a "constitutive outside" which negates it – which amounts to saying that social order never succeeds in entirely constituting itself as an objective social order' (1990: 180). This phrase is derived from Staten's account of the relation between Wittgenstein and Derrida (1984: 16–19). It refers to the non-essential ground of a concept *necessary* for conceptuality which, as a limit, prevents its closure and constitutes its condition of possibility. This is codified as the 'essential law of impurity'. In other words, it is a property of concepts. Yet in taking up this phrase it is never determined whether concepts enjoy antagonistic relations, or what these relations might be with. Rather, the phrase only makes sense in so far as the conceptual ideality of society is presupposed and the effects of this ideality can be predetermined. Hence the reliance on the use of representation, although to whom this representation is directed is not stated. The function of the representation is to police the line of social order, to provide instruction in its use. If antagonism is set up in this way, one can only conclude that it only prevents the closure of the theory in which it is articulated. In this sense antagonism is its internal limit. We return to the question of the nature of antagonism in a following chapter.

This question is re-posed if we consider the possibility of producing a topography of polemic in the double sense of *topos*: a designated place to which enunciation is assigned and the specialized rhetorical sense of a 'doctrine of the places', or places one might occupy in argument. One way of doing this might be by formalizing certain styles or codes of address as polemical, in the sense that anthropologists or linguists codify greetings or insults. In doing so, such styles would quickly lose their purpose and their place in proportion to the extent that they become familiar and ideal. This was the fate of the classical manuals of rhetoric and argumentation that rapidly became merely procedures for performing allegiance to a doctrine or position rather than reflections on how it was possible for such positions to be open to dispute. In fact, they only ever really worked as displays or spectacles within quite specific institutional settings.[7] Polemic failed through the attempt to codify or prescribe polemic. Hence the emphasis which needs to be placed on polemic as a process or movement. With polemicization, the places or *topoi* of engagement fail precisely because of their commonplace or *orthodox* nature, and it is through this failure that polemicization appears. In the case of Düttman it is *as* an opening of the political in the Heideggerian sense of *Ereignis*, the event of appropriation through which the political comes to presence through unconcealment or *aletheia*.[8] In the case of Rancière it is as a failure of distribution and the contestation of the policing of this distribution through which the *proletarii* appear. In both cases the economy of a topography is dislocated as the absence of its ground is disclosed. The commonplaces lose their currency to the extent that they are both reason and instrument of dispute, such that the codified relation of meaning and force which polemic requires is confounded. The places of enunciation, which, despite being poly-vocal, remain unified precisely because all voices believe themselves in agreement over that which they contend, fail in the moment of enunciation.

This can be illustrated by another example that dislocates the suturing of the distribution of commonplaces on to the geographical and geometrical distribution of power and resource. In other words, it illustrates the double sense of *topos*, of place as commonplace. It comes from a transformation in the rules and procedures that govern immigration to the United Kingdom, a topic overdetermined by Britain's colonial and imperial past. After the last World War Britain encouraged immigration from its former colonies in order to satisfy its demand for labour. The rights of these immigrants were rarely those of full citizenship and were worthless as protection from the ingrained hostility of the indigenous working class as well as more formal discrimination. To manage immigration, and to appease the hostile sentiments of the indigenous working class, the British government instituted what became known as the 'primary purpose rule' in order to satisfy the suspicion that immigrants entered the country on the pretext of marriage to those from the same country of origin who were already domiciled simply in order to gain citizenship and enjoy the economic prosperity of an advanced industrialized nation at the expense of the indigenous working class, either through taking jobs or tax contributions through social security entitlement. In other words, marriage was reduced to a means and not an end in itself. Much of the suspicion fell on the Muslim practice of arranged marriages, whereby the arrangement made between parents of different families to marry their sons and daughters was suspected of being a means to obtain British citizenship, usually on the part of sons. Support for this practice was justified with reference to the dignity of the rights of different cultures and the racist nature of the state in ignoring or denigrating these rights. The argument was that in so far as Britain represented itself as a modern liberal society it should respect these rights.

One of the first measures adopted by the New Labour government in 1997 was to abandon the 'primary purpose rule'. As a consequence, applications by men for entry on the basis of an arranged marriage rose more than twofold from 1,740 in 1995 to 3,510 in 1997. This did not unleash accusations of abusing the immigration system that would have confirmed the truth of the earlier suspicions for which the rule was designed. The numbers were small and in any case the indigenous working class had ceased to care to any significant degree.[9] Instead, something more interesting happened. The practice of arranged marriage emerged as disputed within the Muslim community itself. Muslim women and girls had become accustomed to the liberalized sexual climate of Britain and expected to enjoy its freedoms. Consequently, they refused to agree to arranged marriages and refused to go to Pakistan in order to enable a husband who they had not met to demonstrate to the British High Commission in Islamabad, where applications rose from 255 to 1,132 in the course of a year, that he was in fact married. The matter was no longer a question of denying that immigrants were self-interestedly taking advantage of an opportunity for economic advancement. It became one of human rights. Stories were reported of bounty hunters kidnapping Muslim girls who had gone into hiding to escape, of families drugging and murdering their daughters to prevent shame and dishonour, and of husbands beating and murdering their wives who refused to comply with their desires.The Muslim tradition of women not talking to 'outsiders' led to the supposition that the extent of the problem is higher than officially acknowledged.

Yet the basis for the claim to defend human rights against these abuses was not straightforward. The government refused to get involved, as it felt that it had satisfied the human right of cultural belonging and had demonstrated its commitment to 'multiculturalism'.

A Muslim representative, Jahangir Mohammed, deputy leader of the Muslim Parliament of Great Britain, tried to deflect attention from the issue by blaming the matter on the high level of unemployment amongst Muslims in Britain, but Hannana Siddiqui, of the well-established London-based Southall Black Sisters women's group, expressed the nub of the problem:

> The British government could and should be doing more and their failure to act to help Asian women who are kidnapped and taken abroad to be married is basically racist. They are saying 'we have to be sensitive and not criticise other cultures', but in doing that they are allowing violations of women's human rights to continue.[10]

The option was obvious. Muslim women's defence groups encouraged Muslim girls to report cases of forced marriage to the appropriate authorities. In effect, this was an attempt to reinstitute the 'primary purpose rule' from below. Shamsad Hussain, a representative of one of these groups, expressed the dilemma:

> It is sad that we have to use what we have always viewed as racist legislation to keep these men out, but it is vital that we protect these women's basic human rights. I reckon hundreds of unwanted husbands have been kept out like this.[11]

Let us examine what has happened here. This episode describes a shift or, more accurately, a state of affairs in which names and their sedimented designations have come adrift and remain to be settled. It is not simply a question of strategy, as if a plurality of basic aims have modified themselves under changed circumstances in order better to achieve those aims with which they are identified. The distribution of minority and majority is undermined. The hegemonic articulation of the British State as 'multiculturalist', through which it manages the question of cultural unity by adopting a neutralist stand that abandons all claims to involve itself in such matters, becomes dislocated. The discrete cultural differences with which the variety of cultural experience is celebrated are revealed not to be so distinct. Similarly, the racist nature of this state is now attributed to its indifference and tolerant *laissez-faire* attitude, whereas before it had been a question of deriving its racist nature from its active intervention amongst its immigrant minorities in order to exclude them from the sphere of social visibility. By the same token, one of these minorities takes it upon itself to exercise an instrument that formerly had been constructed to ensure such exclusion; or rather, because this episode bears witness to the non-managed or ungoverned distribution of majorities and minorities, the designation of each is brought into question by the emergence of what we may call an anti-minority within the minority which refuses the game of seeking majority-minority status. The logic of the 'primary purpose rule' is tactically appropriated through improvisation. This situation is reminiscent of what Balibar refers to as the generalization of minority status in which the *distinction between "minorities" and "majorities" becomes blurred* in a number of ways' (1995: 53, original emphasis), as increasingly individuals are less classifiable, and which is linked to a 'global pattern of *internal exclusion*' (55). In this ' "Identities" are less isolated *and* more incompatible, less univocal *and* more antagonistic' (56). Antagonism arises through the emergence of the anonymity of the Muslim girls that cannot be placed. Doubtless, this anonymity will not last long.[12]

This antagonism takes place through a 'measure of incommensurables' – specifically, within the discourse of rights which is to guarantee equality. On the one hand, there is the implementation of cultural rights as a universal principle in order to foster tolerance between different cultures within the same geographical space. This inscribes the principle that all cultures are equal in their difference. On the other, there is the assertion of 'human rights', which curtails the scope of the jurisdiction of the principle of cultural rights in the name of a 'human' equality. Here, equality and the distribution it authorizes is put to the test, polemicized, in order to construct a scene of validity. There is no symmetry between these equalities. Their universality is neither transcendental or essential but established through polemic that puts universality to the test. A subversive equivalence emerges between them that reveals a dimension of dispute that calls the grounds of the engagement into question, or at least reveals its errancy. There are no grounds to secure the dispute, or, what amounts to the same thing, foundations are in dispute. While such a dispute is assumed to take place within a space that is both between the participants and within them as a common and limited space of intelligibility, this is both relied on and brought into question. Grounds are polemicized, which may take the form of the awareness that grounds have to be given or, equally, have to be evaded. Rancière summarizes this process in the following terms:

if there is politics it is because one party does not recognise the other as such, or considers that there is no object of dispute, or that the subjects of the discussion are not constituted. Political argumentation must polemically construct the scene of its validity. (1995a: 177)

1.2 The Commonplace of Political Modernity

What is this politics that arises from a scene of antagonism and construction and which aims to preserve this scene? To answer this we must enter into a dispute between terms which is more than a matter of resolving their definition. These terms are politics and the political. Normally, these enjoy a tautological relationship. Politics refers to the occurrence of a type of activity and names it as such; the political refers to a nominalization of the adjective that describes this type of activity. In naming the political, politics is specified by its location within a specific domain; for example, the business of government, procedures of election, the composition of parties and the like. Modern liberal democracies conceive this domain within the parameters of territorial representation. This domain generally has a public character, or a public is constituted through it, in the sense that there is nothing occult, esoteric or private about it. It is visible for all to see, and all may challenge acts of concealment that occur within it. Doing so is held to be a consequence of the exercise of the right of the individual citizen-voter, which is aligned with a series of other rights through the negotiation over their status and relative weight in particular circumstances. The activity or passivity of the individual citizen is not only a matter of calculation and expediency. It is also a matter of differing ontological commitments in that rights are variously derived from nature and/or historical acquisition, although the issue is rarely disputed in these terms.

From this perspective politics is largely a matter of the distribution or management of power, interests and resources. The sum of the practices of this distribution is usually referred to as the political system and is the object or concern of a political science. This body of knowledge is characterized by the aim of providing confirmation of the objectivity of the political system and has developed various procedures or methods for carrying out this task, most of which derive from positivism and which aspire to satisfy propositional criteria analogous to those that characterize the natural sciences, with variable degrees of success. This is even extended to those beliefs, ideas and values that animate these activities, although this generally occurs through some idealized and abstract account of political agents: for example, in terms of 'common sense' or the notion of individuals as self-interested advantage maximizers independent of situations where such action occurs. In short, politics is relegated to a functional subsystem that has the task of regulating the propriety of the sphere of appearances. Politics is equated with the police – in the sense of policy or governing through the creation of consent for a distribution of shares and a hierarchy of places and functions (Rancière 1995b: 63) – and both are subsumed under the tautology of the political.

This confinement of the political through the epistemological discipline required to satisfy its scientific ambition serves to reinforce the sense of politics as that which occurs within the institutional ensemble of the political regime, even if in fact very little politics actually occurs there other than through day-to-day administrative rivalries or through the transformation of the political process into a spectacle. For these and other reasons the equation between the propositional authority of political science and the authority of the objectivity of the political system has been subjected to a series of criticisms. The requirement that politics exists only if it can be measured has been presented with the problem of the failure of anything like a political object to emerge in a manner which would not in itself be subject to dispute. In general, what gets measured is either behaviour or procedure, although in a very superficial sense, or the distribution of resources or even personnel. Critics of the scientific ambition of political science argue that in fact a process of rationalization or technologization is mistaken for politics itself, and that this process is political in a sense that political science is unable to comprehend. In addition, critics of this proto-science argue that it is secretly normative in that it legitimates whatever state of affairs happens to exist by naturalizing modern liberal governance. Through this critique politics itself becomes politicized. The location of the object is brought into question and the concept of the object is shown to be insufficiently determined, or 'particular', as more recent critics would put it.[13]

The dominant – and some would say dominating – strand of contemporary political philosophy exercises the task of resolving this uncertainty and in this activity it is subordinate to the aspirations of political science. The tautology of the political is reinforced. Against this Lefort's work constitutes a significant and systematic attempt to break with the tautology of the political and overcome the limits of political philosophy through a critique of the ambition of political science to delimit the political as an object – for example, through opposition to the non-political or through the reduction of the political to a particular, and to propose a radically different approach to the political.[14] This is done by identifying the political with the 'principles that generate society or, more accurately, different forms of society' or 'regimes' (1988: 217). Rather than the regulation of appearances, the political is concerned with how these appearances come to appear, the underlying logic of their appearance or principles of their articulation. These are at once of 'internalization', 'differentiation' and 'discrimination', which govern the intelligibility of society, or how it comes to be known, and which cannot be derived from the notion of the limits of the social – a fiction which, as we have already suggested, merely serves to support an objectivist or positivist 'science of society'. They are neither immanent nor the effects of an unknown external cause. Instead, they are understood as the mode of institution of society in the sense of a regime that shapes or gives form to society: a *mise en forme* that implies both making sense of social relations – *mise en sens* – and staging or determining how these relations are to appear – *mise en scène* (1988: 216–20). For example, in the way that asymmetrical power relations are stabilized without recourse to the open exercise of force over the dominated such that they appear as legitimate and in accordance with the nature of things.

Lefort's method of analysis is philosophical. It is derived from the Continental and Marxist traditions, and in particular Merleau-Ponty's distinctions between the visible and the invisible, the body and the flesh. These traditions are generally considered to be inimical to the values of sobriety and common sense that the dominant Anglo-American approach to political philosophy imagines that it upholds.[15] Yet the object of this analysis is historical, or, more specifically, a transformation through and within history from which the political emerges. As Lefort does not propose anything like a theory of historical development or evolution that would subsume history under philosophy, the argument is characterized by a fundamental tension between these two disciplines.[16] Lefort acknowledges this and in doing so poses the question of the limits of both, although this is not finally resolved. The issue that organizes this confrontation concerns the political nature of modernity, what he calls 'historical society *par excellence*'. This is a type of society that 'has the virtue of relating society to the experience of its institution' (1988: 228) and follows from its representation of power as an empty place that 'involves a reference to a society without any positive determination, which cannot be represented by the figure of a community' (227). Lefort locates this in the moment of revolutionary rupture through which sovereign power and the truth that it represents is relocated, from, according to Dallmayr's account, 'a site of overt rule to an absent site (or a site of absent presence)' (1993: 91). The historical basis for this is the dislocation of the symbolic ordering of premodern

European society. Following Kantorowicz (1957), this ordering rested on a double inscription of society according to the symbolic resources of the physical human body. Social order was able to represent 'its unity and its identity to itself as that of a body – a body which found its figuration in the body of the King, or rather identified itself with the King's body, while at the same time attached to it as its head' (Lefort 1986: 302). Hence the king's body was always double: secular and divine, mortal and immortal, individual and collective. As is well known, the king owed this reputation to his complicity with the Christian solution to the problem of Jesus's mortal body, and the relation survived this economy of patronage. Individuals were understood as small bodies that fitted together into one symbolic body – society – secured by the king's body at its head, which was at once both a part and the total social body. Understandably, the easiest way to challenge this structure was through the execution of the king, and if possible through the removal of the unfortunate king's head from his body. In the French Revolution, this is what happened.[17]

The effect of this revolutionary act is twofold: firstly, a 'disincorporation of individuals' through which the emergence of individuals as numbers, or what Rancière calls 'mathematical equality', destroyed the idea of society as a substance, unity or identity; secondly, the delinking of power to a specific body that incarnates the social whole. Through this:

> Power appears as an empty place and those who exercise it as mere mortals who occupy it only temporarily or who could install themselves in it only by force or cunning. There is no law that can be fixed, whose articles cannot be contested, whose foundations are not susceptible of being called into question. Lastly, there is no representation of a centre and of the contours of society: unity cannot now efface social division. Democracy inaugurates the experience of an ungraspable, uncontrollable society in which the people will be said to be sovereign, of course, but whose identity will constantly be open to question, whose identity will remain latent. (304)[18]

For Lefort this demonstrates a gap between the symbolic and the real, between representation and existence. It is the instituting moment or historicity of modernity in that regicide is simultaneously symbolic and real in so far as it produces this distinction. Much of the subsequent argument rests on the fate of this distinction, and in particular the nature of the mode of existence of the symbolic, which for Lefort is intimately bound up with the fate of democracy. If modernity constitutes the space of society as one of originary division this can only be rendered intelligible through reference to an empty symbolic dimension – in other words, through a nostalgia for the body. This is why modernity understands politics as a field of competition between protagonists who lay claim to the exercise of public authority, thus linking the legitimacy of power – the symbolic – to the facticity of conflict – the real. Through this, differences and their oppositions are made intelligible or *staged*. The structure of the symbolic remains in place within modernity as the assumption of a public authority through which political competition is legitimated and unity is articulated. Political modernity is overdetermined by the persistence of the symbolic. This constitutes the internal limit of political modernity. Modernity is constitutively incomplete or impure.

Part of the problem is that at times, as in the above quotation, Lefort appears to equate political modernity with a necessarily democratic ontology of the social. In Lefort's memorable phrase, modernity corresponds to the 'dissolution of the markers of certainty', which introduces a radical indeterminancy into every dimension of the social that is equated with democracy (1988: 17). On closer scrutiny, however, this equation turns out to be equivocal. Democracy is one possibility of political modernity that arises from the production of the distinction between the symbolic and the real; but the moment of this production, in this case when the guillotine makes contact with the neck of the king, is not necessarily democratic. Another possibility could equally arise, which Lefort acknowledges as the totalitarian possibility. Understandably, it is the task of democracy to maintain a gap between the symbolic and the real (1988: 223). It is the task of totalitarianism to do precisely the opposite. Therefore, we would argue that Lefort's concern is actually with political modernity understood as the production of the distinction between the symbolic and the real from which a variety of possible political forms can arise, none of which can necessarily be privileged through historical or philosophical interpretation.[19] This equivocal dimension constitutes the modern concept of the political or, in Heller's phrase, 'the concept of the political as such' (1990: 120). It arises from the inscription of the epochal discovery that political order has no natural or pregiven basis, which amounts to the discovery of order as such (Bauman 1989: 164). Political modernity not only undermines foundations, it is also without any of its own. This does not mean, however, that foundations do not persist or that foundational projects do not arise, or that society exists as 'ungraspable' and 'uncontrollable'. The experience of political modernity is littered with such phenomena. What it does mean is that such foundations will be contingent, non-necessary, the effects of a purely political logic. The limit of Lefort's account of the political concerns a confrontation with the persistence of these foundations, or rather, the modality of their relocation.

We can identify this limit within Lefort's account of democracy itself. Democratic society becomes an object precisely because it is not given by nature or the supernatural order, but this object is not objective in the sense of a social fact independent of the political processes of its construction. This prevents the symbolization of revolutionary rupture as necessarily democratic, or preserves the eventual and indeterminate nature of this rupture. It is because of this that democracy coexists with other political processes. As Lefort points out, many of these aim to fill 'the void created by an indeterminate society', not least through the attempt to determine the fantasy of 'an image of the People-as-One' which resolves the paradoxes of democracy by actually instituting society against the experience of division. As modern revolutionary experience has taught us, the easiest way to do this is by claiming the name of the revolution itself, which tends to produce some notoriously non-democratic effects.[20] On the other hand, Lefort insists that some sort of collective representation is required to prevent the atomization of society into merely individual interests, which Lefort believes is prevented by the question of legitimacy. Legitimacy is the *mise en sens* of modernity. Although legitimacy exposes the contingency of social representation, it also exposes the contingency of the self-representation of individuals and groups in that it demonstrates that the symbolic cannot ultimately be occupied. We would argue that this requires that democracy is not given. It can only exist in the form of a project to prevent social closure through a certain use of the 'empty place of power'. Therefore, there is no necessary relation between democracy and this 'empty place', or modernity as such. In the following section we will consider the consequences of this for thinking about and advocating democracy.

Moreover, the place of power, through which the 'self-externality' of society is manifested and from which society obtains a 'quasi-representation of itself', is empty in the sense that it is not the attribute of a positive content that it incarnates. Thus, it is not power as such that becomes empty but the means through which it is rendered intelligible or known. This amounts to saying that power remains symbolic in the absence of any necessarily privileged content that would occupy it. The symbolic is the visibility or presence of emptiness. This dematerializes the *Other* and thus, by the same token, the

One. Consequently, modern democratic society can only relate to itself 'through the experience of an internal division which proves not to be a *de facto* division, but a division which generates its constitution' (1988: 226).[21] It is division which prevents the illusion of society as *either* immanent to itself *or* externally caused.[22] This does not mean, however, that power 'designates an empty place' as a place of enunciation. Rather, it means that power belongs to no one. It does not presuppose 'the existence of a community whose members discover themselves to be subjects by the very fact of their being members' (226). Instead, society has no positive determination and cannot be represented by the figure of community. Society appears as divided in its relation to the experience of its institution. 'The being of the social vanishes or, more accurately, presents itself in the shape of an endless series of questions' which cannot be closed through reference to a determining certainty (228). Yet this only concerns the ontological dimension of society, the being of society. It has no necessary political consequences. It simply determines the modality through which politics occurs, or is made visible. The problem is that it does not appear as such, or in itself. It is not visible and is without sense or meaning. However, if the being of society cannot be represented as such this does not mean that society cannot be represented. At this point the tensions in Lefort's account between philosophy and history become visible. On the one hand it is necessary to represent society in order to prevent atomization, yet on the other the 'empty place of power' provides the means for doing so. Given the very contingency of revolutionary rupture this coincidence of necessity and circumstance is very fortunate indeed. Hence the tension can be understood in terms of the opposition between ontology and intelligibility.

Might there not be an attempt to domesticate this opposition through the acceptance of the positivist description of politics as a subsystem? On this basis Žižek's psychoanalytical interpretation of Lefort would be justified. This posits that politics as a subsystem represents '*within* society its own forgotten foundations, its genesis in a violent, abyssal act – it represents, within the social space, what must *fall out* if this space is to constitute itself' (1991: 194, original emphasis). This eruption of negativity corresponds to what Žižek calls 'the fourth moment of the dialectic', the 'vanishing mediator' that 'enacts its own disappearance' when its work is done; which is to say, negativity works as if nothing has happened. In which case, politics occupies the space formerly taken up by the head of the king, albeit with reduced or separated powers – politics according to liberalism, in fact. This is predicated on the assumption that whatever appears in society does so on the basis of the repression of how it came to appear, and thus that what appears is the symptom which represses the decision or 'abyssal act' that institutes society.[23] Yet Žižek's reading can only make sense in so far as social closure is assumed to have taken place, as distinct from being symbolized.[24] In this it enunciates the perspective of the police, or at least that which would correspond to the unconscious of the police. This is because Lefort's notion of the political undermines the notion of the self-constitution of society, or society as an institution instituted through the distribution of appearances, or the symbolic as such. Political modernity institutes the principle of society's undoing. Naturally, no institution can institute this.

Dallmayr has grasped the logic of the underlying tension in Lefort's argument in the following very precise terms:

> In the face of modern democracy, political thought is caught on the horns of this dilemma: either it must reinvest democracy with traditional metaphysical symbolism, thereby obscuring its novelty, or else cancel all modes of symbolization, at the risk of ignoring the political (as generative space). (1993: 95)

For example, Lefort insists that the fact that the space of modernity 'is organized as *one* despite (or because of) its multiple divisions and that it is organized as *the same* in all its multiple dimensions implies a reference to a place from which it can be seen, read and named' (1988: 225). Aside from the question of whether this is the case, this suggests that the political is conceived as an external point or cause that institutes society on the model of a prime mover or creative God of which philosophy provides knowledge of 'the One' through reflection. Power simply occupies this place in God's absence, although there is no predetermined candidate who would exercise it. It is as if the rupture of modernity never happened. Moreover, the necessity of the thought of the One would appear to find its empirical verification in such notions as state, people, fatherland, even humanity itself. In this, philosophy coincides with and grounds a politics which it understands as radically other than itself, reproducing the tautology of the political. These notions can either sustain the argument that social being remains grounded in the religious, or that social being has become religious. Although Lefort suggests that in fact the unity of these notions is something that has been grafted or projected on to the experience of their indeterminancy, Lefort also argues that it is necessary to do so and is therefore inevitable. In this Lefort's thought is constrained by the inheritance of *ontotheology*, even as it confronts it.[25]

In short, it is the persistence of the religious element, or the premodern articulation of religion and politics in the form of a nostalgia for the body, that makes it possible to refer to society as a stabilized and ordered entity at all. In other words, the persistence of religion provides a dimension of necessity in the form of the symbolic as that which 'governs access to the world' or makes it intelligible. According to this argument, which perhaps relies too heavily on anthropological orthodoxy, there is no other way that this dimension of *mise en sens* can occur except through the symbolic, as it is this which provides the spatial and temporal continuity that allows one to refer to anything resembling a society. Matters are made more difficult with Lefort's insistence that both philosophy and religion are concerned with 'the excess of being over appearance', which undermines the 'illusion of pure self-immanence', with the qualification that for religion this concern is more authentic. Even scepticism is only intelligible through the assumption of one true knowledge at which it aims. In this, philosophy retreats from thinking the experience of division, fragmentation and heterogeneity even as it corrects the illusion that society is self-grounding. Therefore, the persistence of religion in the form of the symbolic undermines the integrity of both democracy and philosophy as it defeats the modern ambition to be self-organizing and self-comprehending. To overcome this subordinate position philosophy is faced with the task of confronting the problem of 'the representation of a form of power which has no religious basis' (224).

Given this dilemma, we would pose the following question. Is the persistence of the symbolic a characteristic of modernity or is it a characteristic of Lefort's argument? In other words, is it a question of historical facticity or of the limits of the philosophical discourse through which this is understood? Lefort acknowledges this equivocal dimension in the question mark that punctuates the title of the essay in which his account is put forward in its most concentrated form: 'The Permanence of the Theologico-Political?' (1988). The persistence of this diacritical inscription within Lefort's elaboration is decisive, as it prevents the closure of the symbolic, despite its persistence. It is of the nature of an object that cannot ultimately be reduced to a predetermined field of intelligibility. It takes the form of the imperative of a question that remains unanswered. Thus:

> We have to ask how the philosophical idea of the One colludes with the image of a united society. We have to ask why unity must be conceived beneath the sign of the spiritual, and why division must be projected onto the plane of material interest. (229)

We would suggest that this collusion is the ontotheological commonplace of modernity, the reduction of modernity to a discursive and topographical place or community that is assumed to be shared on the basis of an overarching unity or scheme, as if the execution of the king had never taken place.[26] Instead, new candidates emerge as the incarnation of the idea of the One. This is why Lefort cannot answer his question, as to do so would risk explaining away the permanence of the theologico-political that his thought has identified.[27] The displacement of the inscription of the social body does not guarantee its eradication. This remainder is therefore a difficulty that confronts modernity when it attempts to think itself – that is to say, to comprehend the modality of its existence. In doing so it can only turn to the persistence of that which it thought it had displaced because this remains the only available model of thought.

Presented in this manner, it is difficult to avoid the impression that modernity has been elevated to the status of something like an agent or subject that produces necessary effects, or to an established and objective fact from which a series of effects could be deduced. In this self-constitution modernity is inevitably subordinated to the grammar of the dialectic.[28] Yet it is this option that the experience of political modernity prevents. If modernity could be self-determining or objective, which would amount to a paradoxical transparency of indeterminancy, then totalitarianism and fundamentalism would be alien to it. Evidently, this is far from the case. It is the dislocatory effects of modernity that give rise to these phenomena by revealing the contingency of the grounds that they would inscribe. In order to overcome the limits of the thought of these effects, the oscillation of the symbolic and the real, it is this commonplace that should now be interrogated.

1.3 Polemicizing the Commonplace

In his useful and sympathetic critique Dallmayr concludes that Lefort 'does not sufficiently indicate how a post-metaphysical notion of democracy might be conceived and formulated and how, in turn, it might relate to theology – given the latter's nexus with symbolization' (1993: 95). It is true that Lefort does not provide anything like a positive post-metaphysical political doctrine yet this may be because to do so would be a contradiction in terms. It would reproduce the problem that Lefort wishes to overcome, not least in the assumption of the prescriptive and normative efficacy of philosophical discourse itself. Dallmayr's solution to this problem is to turn to the example of the later Heidegger's reconfiguration of philosophy as thinking. Although no one would wish to be complicit with 'the forgetting of Being' if they could possibly help it, this should not be at the expense of a disavowal of the ruptural experience of modernity, to which Heidegger was opposed for political reasons that were markedly non-democratic. Hence we would not import Heidegger's thought whole-sale into the notion of the political, even though we recognize the merit of many of his formulations. Rather, we would suggest that it is perhaps possible to deepen Lefort's question mark through general-izing it. This would preserve philosophy as a practice of ungrounding or strategy of thinking that postpones or interrupts the security of metaphysical certainty. This practice consists of the posing of ques-tions that do not correspond to an enunciative position or belong to a subject. They do not require qualifications to be enunciated. Rather, they are within experience, or part of the world. The important point is that in this practice philosophy polemicizes any relation to an empirical space of politics with which it would coincide, and thus its own commonplace nature. In doing so, it opens the space of another politics, or rather, of the political as opening. What is opened is the propriety of power, the opening that modernity has struggled with in the conflict between the double embodiment of the people and the double embodiment of the king, or the incarnation of its name. Only the anonymity of the *demos* can polemicize the propriety of power as it exceeds its ordered distribution.

For example, it may well be that the people is a pole of identifica-tion, but at all times 'the identity of the people remains latent.' Any discourse that names the people is multiple and thus dissolves the unity that it tries to fix. There is no rule for the ascription or interpretation of such a name other than that which derives from the spatio-temporal presence of competing attempts to fix it. It is this indeterminate aspect which prevents the solidification of the name into religiosity. By the same token, this indeterminacy is not grounds for the dismissal of notions such as the people on the basis that it is evidence of its illusory character, and therefore that one need only refer to the dimension of individuals and coalitions of interests as the real stuff of politics. This simply replaces 'the fiction of unity-in-itself with that of diversity-in-itself' (Lefort 1988: 232). Through this, power is reduced to the real and the 'reference to an empty place gives way to an unbearable image of a real vacuum' that is filled by representations that incarnate social unity. Lefort refers to this as totalitarianism. Social division is denied and society becomes a body.[29] The distance between enunciation and utterance is abolished, 'imprinted on every subject, regardless of the signification of words'. In this way certainty is 'reborn'.

This clarifies Lefort's argument that the modern relation of society to its institution in division is not visible in the sense of an object that could be known, but symbolic in that it produces a series of effects that arise from division. This requires a slightly different sense of the symbolic than the one Lefort settled with. In Lefort's terms, the symbolic prevents the collapse of the saying into the said, or the sayable into the intelligible. For this to be the case, however, the symbolic must be understood as opaque and for which a principle of interpretation is not given but constructed within a conflict of inter- pretations which produce a series of deconstructive effects which prevent the transparency of society.[30] The symbolic is no longer conceived of as an ordered and structured self-referential entity on the religious model in its action or modality, even if it remains so in its self-referential intelligibility. It is fragmented and heterogeneous through its relation to something external to it, the historicity of the division that institutes its emptiness, or the production of the distinction between the symbolic and the real, which is the production of the symbolic as such. There is nothing divine or esoteric about this historicity. It does not secure the objectivity of the social by prescrib- ing the distribution of propriety through which identities could be placed but gives rise to the conflictual processes that characterize political modernity, the contingency of identity itself. The symbolic is therefore the site of a conflict between the experience of division from which it arises and the unity through which it is understood. The symbolic – which ultimately means the police – is concerned above all wth maintaining its unity, the presence of its emptiness. In this case democracy could be understood in terms of the deconstructive effects of these conflicts, and not their legitimacy or lack thereof, in so far as these confound the distinction between unity and diversity, symbolic and real. Democracy works through the aleatory logic of wit.

This emphasizes the equivocal notion of power in Lefort's

argument, which enjoys two senses. Firstly, as an empty place in the sense of a 'void' which competing political projects attempt to occupy by virtue of its position at the apex of the social, but which can never ultimately be filled except through a purely political decision which closes the gap between the symbolic and the real, or totalitarianism. This is the secularized version of the double embodiment of the king. From this perspective power authorizes and mediates. Secondly, power is the emptiness of the symbolic itself, in which power is rendered fragmentary and non-substantial and through which legitimacy and authority can only appear as a series of questions which cannot finally be legitimately and authoritatively answered. This is the ruptural experience of modernity before any secular restoration. From this perspective power subverts and produces. These two senses can be understood in terms of the following question. Are the principles that institute political modernity derived from the secularization of the double inscription of society – the removal of the king's head, which nevertheless leaves intact the symbolic structure which it secured – or from the revolutionary rupture that finds its positive expression in the revelation of the contingency of social order through which mortality is affirmed? In our terms, this is another version of the opposition between the police and the *demos*. Perhaps this is simply a testament to the double inscription of power itself, or at least to the persistence of dead languages, as both *potestas* – power over, or legitimate, authorizing power – and *potentia* – power to, or fugitive, polemicizing power? Neither philosophy nor politics has resolved this question, but at least philosophy has posed it in its essentially aimless manner.

This brings us back to the anonymity of the *proletarii*, of proletarian philosophy. The doctrine of the 'empty place of power' entails not only that power lacks a place. Power is also the movement of displacement of places both rhetorical and topographical, of the commonplace. It is insurgent. In this sense power is 'nonplace as place'. The naming of the *demos* as the attempt to fix and distribute places, to institute the commonplace, should not be seen as non-modern, even if it is resolutely anti-modern. It is modern because it too depends on the power of displacement in the attempt to fix the distribution of appearances. Thus any fixing will be antagonistic. This remains the case, even if such a dependency is disavowed – for example, through recourse to the mystical authority of a prior harmonious state. Such alibis are polemical and not essential. They are simply pragmatic attempts to congeal and conceal power through the rhetoric of the commonplace. In other words, authority is simply the occultation of power.

To conclude, we can return to Rancière's account of the political in terms of the modality of polemic against the police. The political is not simply the presence of power. Nothing is political in itself but requires the presence of the test of equality through which an authoritative distribution of appearances is displaced and the question of the *demos* is opened, brought into dispute – in other words, the presence of that diacritical object that cannot be domesticated within an authoritative distribution of appearances. In this Rancière agrees with Lefort's emphasis on the relation between democracy and indeterminancy, yet deemphasizes Lefort's reference to 'a catastrophe in the symbolic linked to the disembodiment of the "double body" of the king' which takes place in a 'theater of sacrifice' (1998: 100). This is because, if this reference is raised to the level of the essential and necessary, it simply serves to provide the opportunity for the reembodiments of terrorism and totalitarianism and occults the democratic polemic between a social body and 'a body that now displaces any social identification' by revealing the contingency of the former (100). In this case the political is not exhausted by the punctual moment of revolutionary rupture but requires the multiplicity of situations of argument in which appearances are contested. These are instances of 'political invention' that create litigious communities (59). On this basis democracy should not be conceived in terms of a regime or *ethos* but as the disruption of the distribution of appearances, the presence of the more or less than one that tests the equality of this distribution.

That said, Rancière remains in agreement with Lefort's diagnosis of the relation between political philosophy and politics, even going so far as to claim that within modernity 'social science' continues the 'philosophical project of achieving politics by doing away with it' (92). The critique of this development is unrelenting and decisive. Thus:

> To return to pure politics and to the purity of 'political philosophy' today has only one meaning. It means returning to a point this side of the conflict constitutive of modern politics as well as this side of the fundamental conflict between philosophy and politics: a theoretical idyll of a philosophical determination of the good that the political community would then have the task of achieving; a political idyll of achieving the common good by an enlightened government of elites buoyed by the confidence of the masses. The 'philosophical' return of politics and its sociological 'end' are one and the same. (93)

The remainder of this book is concerned with the task of polemicizing this happy coincidence – that is, with the work of getting to *that* side.

Notes

1. Düttman explores this insight in his exceptional book, *At Odds with Aids* (1996), which affirms the 'disunity' of existence against a teleology of loss.
2. Rancière also writes:

   > it is that the people are always more or less than they are supposed to be: the majority instead of the assembly, the assembly instead of the community, the poor instead of the city, applause instead of agreement, pebbles counted instead of a firm decision taken. Reaching a decision by totting up pebbles and the bemoaning of the stupidity of majorities are the small change of that 'one too many', that divergence from itself, which constitutes the *demos* as such. The people are at once disproportionate and anarchic. (1995c: 94)

3. This last sentence corrects the view of Kantorowicz (1957). We come back to this in the following section in our discussion of Lefort.
4. In fact, as *proletarii* is a Latin term Rancière does not provide an exact Greek equivalent; *ochlos* only approximates its sense. Instead he refers to the proximity of the sea in the context of Classical Athenian politics, designating Platonism as an 'anti-maritime polemic'. For Plato,

   > the sea smells bad. This is not because of the mud, however. The sea smells of sailors, it smells of democracy. The task of philosophy is to found a different politics, a politics of conversion which turns its back on the sea. (1995c: 2)

   For us this mixing of times and languages is perfectly consistent with the idiomatic dimension of polemic.
5. It is normal in political thought to distinguish these as commutative and distributive justice.
6. Obviously, Marx misdirected himself in turning the proletariat into a pole of identification. That is, he assigned it a proper place, a name. That this reification did not help matters at all is evidenced by the series of substitutions which it initiated: party, class consciousness, 'heroic worker', etc. – in short, the domestication of the proletariat within the distribution of appearances.

7. This refers to the ancient dispute over whether rhetoric was to be considered descriptive or prescriptive in so far as it was possible to formalize it in any systematic manner. In Europe, from at least the Middle Ages, rhetoric became increasingly associated with the figures of discourse and was reduced to the display of *elocutio* at the expense of the expansion of the genres of rhetoric – deliberative, judicial, epidictic. Genette summarizes this process as a *'generalized restriction'* (1982: 104).

8. For an analysis of Heidegger's work that creates a concept of the political out of these terms, see Schürmann (1987).

9. This is not to deny the persistence and increase of racist attacks in Britain. Support for such attacks is usually muted although often overlooked by the police. The most brutal of these concerns the murder of Afro-Caribbean teenager Stephen Lawrence in 1993 at a London suburban bus-stop by five white youths. These youths have been widely identified in the media but never successfully tried, largely because of police indifference and institutionalized racism in the investigation of the case.

10. 'Huge Rise in Forced Marriages', *The Independent*, 20 July 1998.

11. 'Bounty Hunters Tail Runaway Brides', *The Independent*, 20 July 1998.

12. Of course, this is a further instance of the question 'Can the subaltern speak?', formulated and addressed in the work of Spivak. See Guha and Spivak (1989).

13. In saying this we are not saying anything new, and we are not saying it in an extremely summary form. As most readers are aware, arguments such as these have long been associated with thinkers such as Oakeshott, Arendt, Wolin and Connolly. Even Marxists have made these criticisms, but on the whole to the end of an anti-politics.

14. 'Science deals only with particulars' (Lefort 1988: 217).

15. For good introductions to Lefort, see Howard (1977) and Thompson (1984).

16. In fact, in the essay 'Marx: One Vision of History to Another', Lefort characterizes Marx's thought as 'divided' between a continuous logic of history and a discontinuous logic of political events. Rather than dismiss Marx, Lefort opens the trajectory of this division in which he locates Marx's achievement (1986: 139–80). In our elaboration of the political we will apply this same principle of reading to Lefort.

17. It had happened earlier in England in 1649 with very different consequences.

18. For us, this can be seen as the basis of Rancière's position, although he gets it from Aristotle.

19. In fact these are discussed under the title of Lefort's 1986 book: *The Political Forms of Modern Society*.

20. Of course, Lefort acknowledges this in his discussion of the conflict between Robespierre and Danton. Yet the main focus of Lefort's essay is with those nineteenth-century French historians such as Michelet who were confronted with the problem of the Revolution. According to Lefort, these writers attempted to reformulate the principle of the 'Royalty of Spirit' within the Revolution itself (1988: 254).

21. In this the relation between power and conflict is radically reversed, undermining its misrecognition in the liberal contractarian tradition. 'The institutionalization of conflict is not within the remit of power; it is rather that power depends upon the institutionalization of conflict' (226).

22. Lefort adds an important paragraph that illustrates the empirical consequences of this principle of the political. Thus:

> It should be added that, once it has lost its double reference to the *Other* and to the *One*, power can no longer condense the principle of Law and the principle of Knowledge within itself. It therefore appears to be limited. And it therefore opens up the possibility of relations and actions which, in various realms and in particular in those of production and exchange, can be ordered in terms of norms and in accordance with specific goals. (226)

23. In accordance with the Freudian psychosocial principle of reading, Žižek simply analogizes everything to the myth of primal patricide.

24. Here Žižek reiterates his earlier dialectical interpretation of Lefort through which political modernity is reconciled with the Hegelian account of the holy as an empty place filled in by created appearance. Through this the political is subsumed under the logic of filling a void, rather than creating one (Žižek 1988: 147, 194).

25. Ontotheology refers to the metaphysical approach that derives order from a unified or singular ground that functions as a governing principle. In other words, ontotheology is the combination of the axiomatic with the axiological in order to construct a totalizable system. For an account of the evolution of this concept from Kant to Heidegger, see Hart (1989: 75–96).

26. Of course, it was Foucault who endeavoured to conceptualize a politics that had accepted this fact in the movement from a *symbolics* to an *analytics* of power. For example: 'At bottom, despite the differences in epochs and objectives, the representation of power has remained under the spell of monarchy. In political thought and analysis, we still have not cut off the head of the king' (1978: 88–9). In this Foucault's project strives to overcome the belated relation of philosophy to politics by articulating a politics which philosophy cannot think, and which by the same token neither can politics conceived as a subsystem

27. In a sense, Foucault is guilty of having done this.

28. For a defence of the inevitability of this option, see Pippin (1991, 1997). For the opposite view see Kolb (1986).

29. Lefort adds:

> And, it should be noted in passing, we find here an explanation as to why so many contemporary philosophers – and by no means minor figures – have become compromised in the adventure of Nazism, fascism or communism; the attachment to the religious which we noted earlier traps them in the illusion that unity and identity can be restored as such, and they see signs of its advent in the *union* of the social body. It is not because they submit to a charismatic authority that they lend their support to totalitarian regimes, particularly not if they rally to communism; they surrender to the attraction of a renewed certainty and, paradoxically, they use it as a pretext to assert their right to contemplate freely the basis of any experience of the world. (233–4)

Lefort's essay was originally published in France in 1981.

30. This moves Lefort closer to Nietzsche's doctrine of a 'war of interpretations' than perhaps he would otherwise have liked.

Chapter 2

Polemicization and Political Philosophy

2.1 Polemicization and Attitude

The common sense of philosophy is that the distinctiveness of philosophical discourse is located in the assumption that the resolution of
dispute will issue in unaminous agreement. The knowledge of forms,
the certainty of reason or the method of verification all assume that the
purpose of dispute is to arrive at conclusions that are themselves
beyond dispute. Of course, this does not explain the coexistence of
rival philosophical doctrines happily engaged in the pursuit of their
respective universality, although it does suggest that the primary
assumption of univocity is unfounded. Within philosophy there is
no account of this state of affairs in terms other than the privation of
philosophy itself. This is curious, as in many ways dispute constitutes
the productive and inventive dimension of philosophy. It is as if
through dispute philosophy appears to have discovered itself in breach
of its own rules. These rules for the conduct of philosophy stretch back
at least as far as the opposition that philosophy determined between
itself and rhetoric. Rhetoric was taken to be unreliable, if not corrupt,
because of its dependency on a concrete context for its intelligibility.
Yet rhetoric enjoyed the advantage of practical effect. Somewhat
perversely, philosophy came to be most at home with itself when
most impractical, or, to use Hume's term, 'impotent'.

This background lies behind the lingering suspicion that 'political
philosophy' is a contradiction in terms, or that either term is inadequate to the demands of the other. Since the disappointment of the
hope that rulers would become philosophers became a common theme
of philosophy, the aims of political philosophy have always been
limited by the knowledge that the world is not philosophical enough
for it. After all, if it was, its task would be redundant. In addition,

without the receptive ear of an established ruler that could be relied upon, the question of the addressee of political philosophy has always been unresolved. Even those philosophies that propose that one should minimize one's expectations about the conduct of political actors in order to increase the chances of finding its views accepted discover that, for example, individuals are not self-interest-maximizing enough, or enough of the time, to comprehend their actions; or indeed that, contrary to what Hobbes thought, life is not 'nasty, brutish and short' enough to warrant a reconsideration of the basis of social membership. This is because political philosophy proceeds on the basis of a relation between itself and a political field which normally it attempts to master, yet little is said about this relation. It has acquired the sense of the obvious, even in those criticisms of this relation which accuse philosophy of idealism. Such criticisms in fact pay a compliment to philosophy in that it is confirmed in its self-image as playing by its own rules and playing on a field of superior quality. At the same time, within the conditions of its enunciation, this compliment is returned to the critic in that politics is given as somehow beyond philosophy or other to it. In other words, the obviousness of the relation is reinstalled such that, to borrow a term from Heidegger, the relation has become *sclerotic*. The relation proceeds as if nothing happens and both sides find themselves secured by it. By this we mean that the belief that there are in fact opposed sides is confirmed.

According to Rancière, this relation has been fraught right from the start on account of philosophy's somewhat belated relation to politics. That is to say, politics is reduced to the level of epiphenomena of a centre that is both ground and origin of the rule of the One. In this, 'Philosophy thus puts an end to the political, by employing metaphorical resources which at once distance it utterly from empirical politics and allow it to coincide exactly with it' (1995c: 15). This denial is internal to political philosophy.[1] It puts an end to those political divisions from which politics arises, representing them as, for example, a corruption or a lack of analytical rigour. In this, philosophy solves the problem of politics for it. It is commonly expressed as the attempt to deduce the political community from the philosophical idea of a ground that can be manifested in a community – for example, as the common good. It is this notion of a ground that unifies politics and philosophy at that moment when they would appear to be most distant – on the one hand idealism, the truth that can only be grasped by looking directly into the sun, on the other hand empiricism, the truth that arises from the experience of power. Both assume an originary homogeneity, a principle that could be incarnated across the political terrain that unifies a centre with a periphery in the same moment in which this distinction is instituted. In this both philosophy and politics are reduced to the level of the police. Arguing against this Platonic heritage, Rancière writes:

> The basis of the politics of the philosophers is the identity of the principle of politics as an activity with that of the police as a way of determining the partition of the perceptible that defines the lot of individuals and parties. (1998: 63)

This is not to say that one should therefore abandon philosophy in favour of the urgency of a realism that political science seeks to impose in its equation of reality with what it takes to be the empirical existence of politics. To do so would be to reproduce the tautology of politics and the distribution of the perceptible, this time not from the standpoint of philosophy but from the facticity of politics as the experience of power. It assumes that which has to be proven: namely, the unity of existence, politics at the level of the One. This assumption forecloses the various ways in which the verification of the claims of political science have been contested in order to open up the empirical terrain of politics – for example, by the reduction of politics to a method of its representation. The contestation takes place precisely because of the coincidence of philosophy and politics, which means that the scientific description of appearances is at the same time a means for verifying their distribution. The point is not to contest the claims of political science concerning the nature of politics, or to derive a superior account of this nature from an innovative political philosophy. Rather, we propose to take a different tack. We aim to show the internal limit of the relation between philosophy and politics within philosophical discourse. This limit concerns above all the supposed opposition between the metaphysical and the empirical, or where philosophy and politics coincide at the point at which each imagines itself to be located at a point of absolute distance from the other. It is at this limit that we locate polemic.

Let us clarify some points to avoid misunderstandings and to flesh out what is at stake in this affirmation that polemic is located in the tension between philosophy and politics, at least within philosophical discourse. Indeed, we do not wish to be seen to be locating polemic within the resources of that which philosophy has traditionally seen as its other: rhetoric. Rather, we wish to pose the question of being polemical. One need only recall the subtitle to *On the Genealogy of Morals – A Polemic (Eine Streitschrift)* – in order to acknowledge the centrality of polemical intention in Nietzsche's work, and which is expressed in his distinctive style. However, as an antidote to the enthusiasm that his style has generated, often through the most slavish forms of imitation,[2] it ought to be said that there is something staged about it as it strains for effect. Indeed, it is this which has helped to make Nietzsche's work so acceptable and unremarkable, so commonplace. Nietzsche's voice is always already familiar. This straining is a symptom of a dependency on an opponent that weakens the confrontation precisely because to acknowledge it would undermine the polemic to overturn metaphysics. The sharpest encounters are dulled by their attempt simultaneously to 'prefigure' new rules, and thus the contexts in which these would operate. The remarks on 'woman' demonstrate this perfectly, as does Nietzsche's cantankerous relation to 'modern ideas'. Descombes's deflationary judgement on the legacy of Nietzsche is apt in this respect:

> Every time we seek to give a philosophically articulate form to one of the Nietzschean themes – whether it be the critique of consciousness, suspiciousness, infinite interpretation, or suprahumanity – we are disappointed at finding familiar conceptual frameworks. The critique of consciousness doesn't go beyond Cartesian mind philosophy. The infinite task of interpretation in no way perturbs empiricist language philosophy. The superior individual is inconceivable outside the idealist philosophy of autonomy. (1997: 90)[3]

Nietzsche also writes or inscribes the failure of the effects of his polemic, however, and it is this that is perhaps the more interesting effect of his style as it re-iterates the dislocation of his project.[4] Polemic occurs in proportion to the extent that polemical intention fails, which means that polemic does not indicate the mere continuation of a will across that which is heterogeneous to it. If this were the case the simple expression of a will – active or reactive – would be redundant. One would simply be concerned with the omnipotence of power, for which polemic would be superfluous. Polemic does not command. Polemicization takes place precisely because such omnipotence is impossible. Put differently, polemicization arises from the failure of a will over that which is heteronomous to it. The other – in Nietzsche's case metaphysics – persists. Hence Nietzsche's constant complaint about the failure of others to see things in the perspective he proposes. Perhaps this is why Nietzsche sought security in the alibi of not being understood as proof of the truth of his discourse. Thus a process of *autopolemicization* emerges through the failure of this self-serving gesture, and thanks to this the originary questions which Nietzsche condenses remain open and continue to solicit. In so far as this dimension of autopolemicization is recognized, then a reasonable chance remains that Nietzsche can resist both assimilation to a canon and the effacement of the value of his works.[5] This might curtail the tendency of his recent followers to evangelize on his behalf as some sort of truth that shall save 'us', or at least the 'sovereign individual' opposed to everything and answerable to no one. Ideally, the use of Nietzsche should not derive from its truth or falsity.

This suspension of truth or falsity, or the procedure that would derive the criteria with which these questions could be decided from authoritative procedures or traditions, formed the concern of Foucault's later reflections on the purpose of his own work. Significantly, he refused the opportunity to describe this enterprise in terms of polemic, volunteering that he preferred the 'serious play of questions and answers' to the sterile oppositions of polemic precisely because the latter risks nothing and only seeks to confirm itself. By contrast, the patient elucidation of a concept through dialogue and dialectic instantiates rights immanent to the encounter; one can 'remain unconvinced', seek 'more information', 'emphasize' things differently, uphold logical argumentation and consistency, be open to the questioning of the other and question the other. Given the choice, who would not opt for the productivity of philosophy over the intransigence of rhetoric, which, on Foucault's description, proceeds by cashing in tokens that are brought to an encounter merely to eliminate an adversary? Foucault was not inventing this experience. One can easily think of those occasions in which a polemic is staged or rehearsed as a confrontation between commonplaces.

Yet Foucault's concern is not with the clarification of the problems of philosophy but with the relation of the question to community. This takes the form of the elaboration of a community around the experience of the question of itself. Through the experience of the question Foucault outlines the dynamic of a community that has no reliable self-understanding, no core around which it can organize and reflect on itself, nothing in common – for example, in the form of a symbolic through which internal hierarchies are distributed and assigned. It stands under nothing. In these circumstances the coincidence of the fit between philosophy and politics is disrupted. In this Foucault was inspired by the experience of 'France, May '68'. In Foucault's memory at least, this event revealed the limits of all established progressive orthodoxy such that the act of questioning was itself liberated. From this Foucault drew a more general lesson which is expressed as the well-founded doubt as to whether it is 'suitable to place oneself within a "we" in order to assert the principles one recognizes and the values one accepts' (1984a: 385). In this refusal of the 'we' the question exceeds itself and thus the place from which it is enunciated and the context in which its intelligibility would be assured. The *topoi* and *doxa* through which community is sustained are deauthorized, suspending the sense of community as witness to its own commonality and dislocating the presence of the community *to* and *in* which community appeals for verification. In our terms, the One of the community is polemicized.

Instead of holding up his hands in despair at the loss of certainties this entails Foucault suggests deepening and reiterating the truth of this experience. Of course, an appeal to a privileged historical moment as exemplary has its drawbacks, not least the self-congratulatory myths that rely on phrases such as 'you should have been there.' Yet Foucault avoids this problem by inscribing the problematic of the question within the broader logic of modernity itself, an inscription which becomes explicit in two other texts that reactivate the question of enlightenment formulated by Kant (1984b, 1993). For Foucault this is a unique event in which a question is posed to the present of the order of 'What is happening today? What is happening now?' (1993: 10). Through this enunciation belonging is both the belonging *of* the question and belonging *in* question. This aspect enabled a continuity across the trajectory of modernity which was staked out in the following terms:

> I have been seeking to stress that the thread that may connect us with the Enlightenment is not faithfulness to doctrinal elements, but rather the permanent reactivation of an attitude – that is, of a philosophical ethos that could be described as a permanent critique of our historical era. (1984b: 42)

Where Kant had sought to establish the limits of what was thinkable in order to secure the necessity of the enunciation Foucault insists that thinking is to be directed at the 'contemporary limits of the necessary itself'. This takes the form of the objectification of limits through the identification of the impurity of contingency in each universality, beginning with the human. This 'limit attitude' (45) entails that 'the critique of what we are is at one and the same time the historical analysis of the limits that are imposed on us and an experiment with the possibility of going beyond them' (50). Under this 'critical ontology of the present' modernity is no longer understood as epochal, as something with a beginning and end. Foucault accomplishes this not by a rejection of modernity but through its polemicization.

In this chapter we will adopt this 'limit attitude' towards the sclerotic relation between philosophy and politics in order to show how the reflexive presence of polemic disrupts its verification. These discussions should be taken in the nature of experiments in attitude, as exercises rather than as examples that illustrate a thesis. This is because the establishment of limits occurs differently in each case.

2.2 Polemicization and the Political

Firstly, let us take Schmitt, who sought to correct the belatedness of philosophy by asserting the urgency and intensity of political conflict through the figure of the friend/enemy distinction. This was not unmotivated. Schmitt saw this urgency as an antidote to liberalism's 'neutralization' of the political. In doing this he failed to grasp the political or 'decisive' nature of liberalism itself, or what he took to be liberalism. In fact, on our reading, the dimension of political intensity in Schmitt arises not from the existence of a political entity that could antagonize and be antagonized by another political entity, but through the question of the existence of the political entity itself. As we show from Schmitt's text, this question, and thus the nature of the political, has an intrinsically polemical value which cannot be derived from the urgency of action or the reflection of philosophy. Rather, it is derived from a somewhat paradoxical absence of a political entity.

Schmitt sought to establish two things: firstly, that the state presupposed the political, something he insisted on in order to avoid the simple reduction of the political to the state considered as a function that was subordinate to society. The state is simply a form that the 'political entity' takes. This implies that it could take other forms or that the state is not necessarily the political entity, and thus not necessarily the sovereign locus of a decision within the terms of Schmitt's problematic. Secondly, he sought to establish that the political was not a substance but a type of relation. For him the political was autonomous and self-sufficient, or self-grounding, such that it rested on 'its own ultimate distinctions, to which all action with a specifically political meaning can be traced' (1996 [1932]: 26). This was, notoriously, the distinction between friend and enemy whereby the political was conceived as a relation of the friend-enemy type. For the moment our concern is with this second aspect. The reference to an enemy is not an alibi for a bellicose conception of the political. Schmitt was careful to insist that the political should not be reduced to warfare or battle. Rather, it concerns the identification of an enemy through what we might refer to as the tautology of the decision; any decision is sovereign which serves to identify an enemy on the occasion on which it is necessary to do so. The military enemy is simply the most 'intense' experience of the decision, but an enemy need not be a military one. Schmitt referred to such a decision as 'the exception', although it is doubtful if Schmitt had a clear grasp of what this might be, as he regarded it as a necessity for the constitution of the political. What is clear, however, is that Schmitt was concerned to establish the political in terms of a relation where the terms are separated by a border or limit. This limit has a double status. It differentiates the same from the other as other, and therefore contributes to configure the identity of the same, but it is also the mark of the hostility of the relation with the other, for the other is also the enemy of the same.[6] Schmitt is mostly concerned with the latter. That is why for him this limit demonstrates that both terms enjoy an antagonistic relation by virtue of the threat of annihilation each represents to the other. In Schmitt's terms, the enemy is:

> the other, the stranger; and it is sufficient for his nature that he is, in a specially intense way, existentially something different and alien, so that in the extreme case conflicts with him are possible. These can neither be decided by a previously determined general norm nor by the judgement of a disinterested and therefore neutral third party. (27)

We wish to bring into question this account of the political. In the first instance this is through an analysis of the way it is brought into question through Schmitt's own elaboration.[7] This is because Schmitt's account reveals the political within the same, or rather, reveals the political as that which brings the same into question. This is not by way of an exterior threat that could be identified with reference to a limit, but by the impossibility of constituting the same as such. To this end we can mobilize two of Schmitt's own stipulations: firstly, that it is not possible to produce an adequate definition of the political solely by reference to the state in so far as the state and the public institutions are neither self-evident nor possess the monopoly on politics (22); and secondly, that any elaboration of the political is necessarily polemical. It is worth recalling Schmitt's remarks to this effect:

Above all the polemical character determines the use of the word political regardless of whether the adversary is designated as nonpolitical (in the sense of harmless), or vice versa if one wants to disqualify or denounce him as political in order to portray oneself as nonpolitical (in the sense of purely scientific, purely moral, purely juristic, purely aesthetic, purely economic, or on the basis of similar purities) and thereby superior. (31–2)

Not only is the political subordinate to polemic. Polemic relies upon a rhetorical character that can be subsumed under the figure of *paradiastole*. This is a figure of redescription for strategic ends on the basis that the ethical and moral distribution of experience is not given as natural, and therefore that the moral qualities of some actions can be redescribed in terms of their opposites in order to denounce or extenuate them.[8] Yet Schmitt failed to recognize the consequences of this for the purity of the concept of the political itself. This is that the political is not given but has to be established through polemic. The concept itself has no existence outside of a polemical practice and the contemporary conditions of this practice in liberal democracies are such that the non-political enjoys a superiority over the political. Indeed, it was Schmitt's whole intention to rectify this situation which he attributed to the regrettable effects of liberalism. This amounts to the autopolemicization of the concept. Yet if this is the case then the purity of the distinction between friend/enemy on which it rests is not given either – which is to say, that the distinction is produced by the political on the basis of a prior distinction between the political and the non-political that arises through polemic. This means that the political itself, and not simply the state or the public institutions is necessarily not 'self-evident and concrete'.[9] The possibility of the non-political polemicizes the political, and this possibility is a structural component of the grammar of the political itself in that it indicates how it is to be used.

We can conclude from this that two senses of the political emerge through Schmitt's elaboration: firstly, the political as rooted in a straightforward distinction between friend and enemy; and secondly, shadowing this, a distinction between the political and the non-political which polemicizes the former in the sense that all semblance of concreteness which the terms of the distinction may acquire disintegrates. Indeed, this second sense may well be the primary sense of the political in Schmitt, given his stated intention to politicize liberalism on the basis that it had neutralized the political understood as the capacity to distinguish between friend and enemy. This is because the political, *as a concept and as a practice*, is governed by its polemical nature. This polemical nature entails that the occasion of the political is always indeterminate, a matter of dissembling, in so far as it is concerned to make an adversary of the non-political, which may in fact turn out to be the dissemblance of its political nature. Needless to say, this distinction cannot be assured. If it were, the very term political would be redundant, and because of this the political cannot be given primarily as an external relation with an enemy because it depends on a prior relation between adversaries, which in turn presupposes a space of commonality structured according to polemic. This commonality is secured by *the indeterminacy of moral and ethical distribution*.

This is illustrated by Schmitt's elaboration of the categories of friend and enemy within the mode of philosophy. Ultimately these are subsumed under the category of the same, the identical, in their very opposition. On this occasion Schmitt relies on Hegel's definition of the enemy as 'a negated otherness' that makes the enemy exterior to the friend through an equation that is supposed to be reversible. Thus: 'But this negation is mutual and this mutuality of negations has its own concrete existence, as a relation between enemies; this relation of two nothingnesses on both sides bears the danger of war' (Schmitt 1996 [1932]: 63). The other is a nothing on the condition that at the same time the same is a nothing too. For Schmitt this dependence can never be called into question, forever frozen in a moment of the dialectic. Yet without the movement of the dialectic there is no dimension of antagonism, a fact overlooked by Schmitt's assimilation of negation to nothingness. To put it bluntly, the relation of 'two nothingnesses' is more properly characterized as one of mutual indifference, and this mutuality could not be understood in terms of a recognition that would issue in a dialectic, as this would undermine the absolute sovereignty of the decision, its non-dependence on anything mutual. In short, the categories of negation and nothingness do not serve Schmitt's purpose well, as it is not possible, or even pertinent to negate something that is, by definition, already nothing, by something which is equally nothing. Unless, of course, there is something within this sameness of nothing that Schmitt tries to establish which blocks the mutual indifference of others and the self-evident character of the friend.

Perhaps as a concession to pluralism and corporatism, Schmitt inadvertently provides this element by admitting that an entity could be the decisive political entity in so far as it has the capacity to deny 'the enemy quality of a certain adversary', that is, to deny the political status of an adversary. It is an accident in Schmitt's argument in the sense of something that befalls it, but it is also the accidental or non-necessary character of the political itself. This centres on Schmitt's discussion of the ambiguous 'public enemy', which he perceives generally as an external enemy. On the face of it Schmitt wishes to uphold Plato's doctrine that within the public space – in the sense of *domestic* public space – war is not possible but only 'discord'. Given that Schmitt has been at pains to deny the identity between war and the political, this is a peculiar route to take. It is forced on Schmitt by the requirement that the public space exists as stable, uniform and unified, the exact opposite of the conditions in which the political is visible. Yet this is prevented by the presence of polemic, the very term that organizes the use of the concept of the political itself and thus the existence of factions that this presupposes. For Schmitt, not only does this entail that the 'all embracing political unit, the state' is weakened, but also: 'The intensification of internal antagonisms has the effect of weakening the common identity vis-à-vis another state' (32). This introduces another scene into Schmitt's elaboration that concerns everything that his polemic strives to avoid: namely, a rivalry between decisions. This scene is domestic while at the same time calling the possibility of the domestic sphere into question. It is the exception within the limits of his argument, the doubling of the exception. With the admission that it is possible to conceive of a rivalry between decisions, where this rivalry is centred on the verification of the existence of an enemy irrespective of who is to play this role, and thus that no decision is available to decide on which decision will in fact be decisive, the political as a relation of interiority/exteriority is displaced by a prior sense of the political which returns us to the polemical opposition political/non-political.

Here, internal antagonism is located within the category of 'common identity', the existence of which is held to be prior to the political in the sense of the friend/enemy distinction, and which Schmitt maintains is threatened by a 'public enemy' that is always external to the polity in question. One wonders whether this dimension of threat should not more accurately be seen as the moment of the constitution of this 'common identity', and conversely, whether this dimension is internal, a property of internal antagonisms around the decision concerning the 'public enemy'.[10] In this case, the distinction between 'public enemy' and internal antagonism collapses. 'Common identity' has no positive content other than the failure of the purity of the distinction between other and same, friend and enemy, and inside and outside. The clear-cut limit, border or virgule between political and non-political evaporates in Schmitt's recognition that the existence of the state, the entity from which the decision to decide on the decision emanates, requires internal peace and thus the ability to identify the 'domestic enemy' (46–7). Yet the presence of the 'domestic enemy' in an argument that strains itself to distinguish domestic disturbance from external enmity (and therefore from the possibility of war) is either a misnomer or a rhetorical device marshalled by a polemicist whose intention had reached an internal limit. It is not difficult to see why. Schmitt distinguishes the private *inimicus* from the public *hostis*, and claims that the political enemy can only be the public enemy. We have seen, however, that he also conceives the latter as an external other, or more precisely, that he would like to reduce it to another sovereign state, so he is forced to describe this peculiar 'domestic' enemy as a *non-political* one. The 'domestic enemy' can only be considered non-political in the polemical sense because the distinction political/non-political is not given except through polemical redescription. For Schmitt it has no rights and is essentially lawless, as distinct from the 'public enemy' or other who may even be a trading partner. It requires an antagonistic scene of verification precisely because the possibility of its existence dislocates the scene of its enunciation. It is this which is the matter of dispute and which cannot be resolved by reference to the authority of a place or a position, a *topos,* as this would be to invoke a decision that has both already taken place and never takes place. Given Schmitt's insistence on the necessity of producing 'enemies' for the sake of a 'common identity', it is questionable whether they exist at all except at the level of fantasy, a dimension notoriously difficult to isolate with any measure of precision. Schmitt's procedure is commonplace. This is why, as Derrida points out, Schmitt follows Plato in only being able to theorize war under the experience of domestic divisions that are exteriorized, othered, at both the theoretical and empirical levels (1997: 114).

One could, of course, use Schmitt himself to bring into question the non-political status of the domestic enemy and dissociate the production of identity from the level of fantasy – for example, by invoking his initial claims: namely, that the concept of the state presupposes that of the political and that the political is a type of relation in which collectivities face one another as friends or enemies. It is true that he maintained that the public enemy is or should be another sovereign state. This was partly due to his nostalgic yearning for a mythical time when clear and distinct political entities faced one another in an interstate system, and to his conservative perception of political order as that which excluded divisions. If he admits, however, that the friend-enemy oppositions that characterize the political are not reducible to their state form, to oppositions between sovereign states, then there is no reason why they couldn't be predicated of antagonisms between political parties or other collectivities within the domestic scene – that is, inside the political order, within the same, or within the liberalism to which Schmitt was opposed. With this possibility the 'common identity' is polemicized, as political oppositions become a constitutive dimension of the domestic scene in so far as these entities remain latent, alien to the distribution of appearances. The presence of antagonism within the same shows the impossibility of constituting a common identity as stable and unified, of portraying the same as an indivisible One, as the oneness of the One. More precisely, in so far as every space of commonality is governed by polemic, it is always already fissured and therefore can only exist in an essentially impure fashion.

Something similar can be seen when we examine the status of the decision in his work. Polemicization demonstrates that the premium traditionally placed on the category of the decision is exaggerated, especially in so far as one would attempt to link this category to the notion of rule. This emphasis and the motivation behind it derive from the legacy of an ontotheological inheritance that informs Schmitt's project. This ontotheological inheritance is most apparent in Schmitt's account of secularization through which he understands the state. Thus: 'The juridic formulas of the omnipotence of the state are, in fact, only superficial secularizations of theological formulas of the omnipotence of God' (42) – specifically, the interventionist God who necessarily decides to create the world. This God is the source of Schmitt's model of the decision. The consequences of Schmitt's reliance on the ontotheology of decision require a further elaboration as it is through these that the coincidence of philosophy and politics in the assumption of the One is effected. In his critique of Schmitt over the wider thesis of *Political Theology* (1985 [1922, 1934]) Blumenberg argued that through the category of secularization Schmitt gets things the wrong way round. For Blumenberg, religion is a political invention. Moreover, in equating genesis with structure the very exception on which Schmitt's notion of the decision relies loses its force as the political is understood as a repetition or imitation of the (onto-)theological, whereas in fact the recourse to theology within political discourse is simply a strategy of legitimation. Thus for Blumenberg nothing actually happens within Schmitt's account of the political. No decision will ever be taken, precisely because, in our terms, it would risk opening the space of decision to polemicization. Thus, on Blumenberg's account:

> decisionism 'lives' from the fact that the 'decisions' have always already been made, that they appear in the form of historical authorities, just as for Hobbes the contract of subjection can never be one that is yet to be sealed, but is only one that is inferred to have gone before. (1983: 98)[11]

In other words, decisionism cannot account for the practices of opposition in response to which decisionism is set up. Perhaps it is for this reason that in response to the challenge to historically conferred authority it gazes upwards to theology. At best, such a conceptual reduction of the political, an originary domestication of the political through the presupposition of an inside and an outside, reduces the political to a subsystem: politics.[12] Against this, we would argue that the political refers to an errancy of the line or the limit. As this is not a matter of enunciation or of decision, although both these terms are bound up within it, we refer to this as polemicization, the process in which this occurs. The issue is more accurately posed as that of the status of the decision in an undecidable terrain. Polemicization involves transitivity. This provides some sense for the paradox of 'hyperpoliticization' that Derrida finds in Schmitt's critique of modernity's 'neutralization' of the political: 'The less politics there is, the more there is, the less enemies there are, the more there are' (1997: 129).[13] In the following discussion of Kant we will examine modernity's production of enemies. This occurs through the polemicization of the authority of rule itself.

2.3 Polemicization and Critique

In contrast, Kant represents the extreme antithesis of Schmitt in that practical action was to be subordinated to and regulated by transcendental ethics organized around the value of autonomy. Yet Kant's whole enterprise is an intervention which seeks not only to communicate the necessity of this value but also to transform the conditions of action such that this value can exist against those which Kant identifies as opposed to it. In this respect critique and the possibility of enlightenment constitute a machine for the production of enemies rather than a pole of identification for one's friends; or rather, enlightenment is a device for the continuation of politics by other means. The space of critique is irreducibly antagonistic. Although Kant seeks to reconcile the antagonistic production of this space with his ethical project, this fails through its reliance on the contingency and heterogeneity of polemic; or rather, polemic fills a gap between the transcendental and the empirical, or the space of practical application. In this, polemic remains unregulated as it cannot be reconciled with the force of empirical or natural necessity, or the requirement that any possible object of experience must be accounted for by its transcendental conditions. We argue that with Kant these elements are subordinate to an interest in polemic.

An interpretation of this nature may strike one as merely perverse or eccentric, as nothing more than a predictable reversal through the application of deconstructive method in which the marginal is elevated to the essential. It is usual to assume that Kant's political philosophy derives from the procedures which governed Kant's critical project. The subordination of social organization to the authority of reason embodied in the sovereign and autonomous rational individual is generally taken to be the way that this should be done. The authority of decision would be preserved through this. In his most systematic statement of political philosophy the 'categorical imperative' – '*Act only on that maxim through which you can at the same time will that it should become a universal law*' – heralds the arrival of the Kingdom of Ends in which a rational being will enjoy its intrinsic dignity as both head and member.[14] Here, philosophy and politics will be at their closest. In its pursuit of autonomy the will of the noumenal self will coincide with the heteronomic acts of the phenomenal self, distributing law and institutions according to reason. The point of departure for our interpretation is the following question: if, as is generally agreed, Kant's critical project was halted by the problem of access to the 'thing in itself' and the distinction between the noumenal and the phenomenal which governs this question, then does this problem apply to its political aspect?

One of the most devastating critiques of Kant's project has recently been reiterated by Honig (1993), following Kelly (1969). Kant allows a purpose for the heteronomic phenomenal realm that can never strictly be reconciled with the priority of the noumenal, rendering it dependent on the heteronomy it seeks to overcome. Thus Kant assumes 'an expressive correspondence between his moral political order and the noumenal self' (Honig 1993: 39). This expressive dimension, which is not accounted for by Kant, provides the link between philosophy and politics. Yet Honig assumes that this assumption, and thus the Kingdom of Ends, has the status of fact in so far as it enables those who do not meet Kant's exacting standards of reason to be relegated to the status of the phenomenal and contingent. This is the relevance of Honig's decision to affirm various attitudes of *virtù* which esteems 'the vitality in a self which exceeds all orderings' and which 'denaturalizes existing arrangements and signals the possibility of alternative ethical and political ideals' (39). *Virtù* is assigned to those whom Kant is supposed to have excluded, the issue of whether exclusion demonstrates the 'vitality' or excessiveness of the excluded notwithstanding.

In making this criticism perhaps Honig goes both too far and not far enough. The argument goes too far in that nothing can be derived from the fact of 'vitality', except perhaps a pulse, but certainly not 'alternative ethical and political ideals'. If there is one advantage to be had from 'vitality' it is that for this phenomenon ideals are superfluous. Indeed, more often than not, 'vitality' signals the ability to be indifferent to ideals, unless of course 'vitality' is itself elevated to the level of the ideal. This is unobjectionable in itself although doing so tends to signal a lack of either. More importantly, the argument does not go far enough in that Kant himself admits that the 'Kingdom of Ends' is unattainable. The ultimate satisfaction of reason can only be given under the condition of an interminable postponement in its search for unconditioned necessity which would ground the coincidence of the universality of law and the autonomy of the will. So Kant can hardly be accused of actually having excluded anything. He can, however, be accused of having undermined the objectivity of the distinction between inclusion and exclusion. For us this is no reason to beat Kant with the club of moral sentiment – quite the opposite, in fact. This is because Kant's argument is designed to support a project. Kant insisted that enlightenment was to be understood above all as a process. For this reason he could not say that he lived in an enlightened age but in an 'age of enlightenment' characterized by openness. This prevents its reduction to a stable referent or an object of experience.

If, however, the 'Kingdom of Ends' does not actually take place, a fact that one could easily verify by reading a newspaper, its inscription within Kant's project does. The nature of this project is indicated by the curious fact that in reaching such an inconclusive conclusion Kant saw no grounds for despair or reproach, as it vindicated his critical enterprise. Thus:

Hence reason unrestingly seeks the unconditionally necessary and sees itself compelled to assume this without any means of making it comprehensible – happy enough if only it can find a concept compatible with this presupposition. Thus it is no discredit to our deduction of the supreme principle of morality, but rather a reproach which must be brought against reason as such, that it cannot make comprehensible the absolute necessity of an unconditional practical law (such as the categorical imperative must be).

Kant concludes:

And thus, while we do not comprehend the practical unconditioned necessity of the moral imperative, we do comprehend its *incomprehensibility*. This is all that can fairly be asked of a philosophy which presses forward in its principles to the very limit of human reason. (Kant 1989: 123)

This happiness, in which reason is only at home with itself in so far as it can comprehend that it has limits distinct from those limits which it seeks to overcome, is indicative of the rhetorical and practical nature of Kant's thought. Kant was well aware that the determination of the limits of what can be known does not by itself determine the limits of what can be done. Kant presupposes that practical matters are ungovernable by reason. In this he accepts the claim concerning the 'impotence' of reason but resists the consequences which Hume drew from this: namely, the elevation of the conserving force of tradition and propriety. After all, Kant's critical project only sought to demonstrate the intrinsic necessity of reason and not the necessity of its consequences. Thus, in becoming practical reason confronts its own limits. As we shall argue, Kant comprehends these limits through the notion of polemic. Polemic is the practical dimension of Kant's project. In the recognition of 'incomprehensibility' the ideal and practice of reason conflict, each limiting the other through their subordination to antinomic demands as if each were to legislate for the other as a prior condition of self-legislation. In this, the inherited relation between philosophy and politics is confounded. Here we would endorse O'Neill's opinion, following Arendt (1982), that Kant's 'entire critical enterprise has a political character' (O'Neill 1986: 524), adding only that this 'political character' is an internal limit. It prevents the completion of the subject, the non-coincidence of the noumenal and phenomenal, and thus renders subjectivity interminable. It is here that polemic is located.

At this point we should consider the nature of the space in which this is supposed to take place. The atmosphere of this space is indicated by Kant's insistence in *The Critique of Pure Reason*[15] that 'skeptical polemic' should only be directed at the dogmatist: 'it should be designed simply to put him out of countenance and thus to bring him to self-knowledge' (Kant 1929 [1781]: 609). Polemic is an agent of the 'complete system of pure reason' opposed to 'a whole system of illusions and fallacies' of which 'ontotheology' has previously been marked as the primary casualty.[16] The aim of this agent is freedom. It is a wholly negative enterprise that will 'expose the illusions of a reason that forgets its limits' in the name of 'modest but thorough self-knowledge' (591). This freedom is the only rule. Self-knowledge, reason, cannot itself be limited with respect to a certain 'freedom of criticism' which it undertakes towards itself and which 'knows no respect for persons' (593). In this task polemic is interminable. It puts freedom to the test. This is justified as resistance to dogma, the orthodoxy that community is a referent, in order to increase the chances of freedom. Common sense, the sense of community as being-with-others, is not a referent but something constituted through polemic. There is no necessary consequence of polemic other than the destruction of dogma and the assertion of the freedom to do so. In this Kant maintains that only the 'critique of pure reason' can be regarded as:

> the true tribunal for all disputes of pure reason; for it is not involved in these disputes – disputes which are immediately concerned with objects – but is directed to the determining and estimating of the rights of reason in general, in accordance with the principles of their first institution. (601)

Nowhere does Kant describe this first institution. This is because the advantage of 'transcendental critique' is that it is 'incompetent to arrive at affirmative assertions'. Only on this basis is critique exterior to polemic as it deals with issues 'outside the field of possible experience'. Thus: 'There is, therefore, properly speaking, no polemic in the field of pure reason' (604). This means that Kant speaks improperly, and will have to do so in so far as polemic aims to create the conditions of proper or free speech, or pure reason. In fact, as this has yet to exist it will never be evident whether Kant is speaking properly or improperly; or rather, only in so far as Kant's discourse is 'incompetent' will it be pure. This means that the competence of Kant's discourse is the measure of its freedom.

If we turn to Kant's more interventionist writings we can acquire a more empirical grasp of this space, albeit through the filter of Kant's imagination. In his famous essay 'An Answer to the Question: "What is Enlightenment?"' (Kant 1991a [1784]) Kant defined enlightenment in a manner that announces a polemical intent under the slogan 'dare to think.' Enlightenment aims to 'put out of countenance' in a manner which pays no respect to the sensitivities of others. Thus: '*Enlightenment is man's emergence from his self-incurred immaturity*' (1991a: 54). Maturity is a matter of a courageous and resolute posture. Maturity is autonomy. It affirms a confidence in one's own capacity for understanding and a rejection of the authority of others in matters of knowledge. Fear, laziness and cowardice keep the general run of mankind in its place simply because this is how it would prefer to be, gladly subjecting itself to dogmas and formulas, the 'ball and chain of its permanent immaturity'.[17] As O'Neill (1986) points out, Kant is not like other liberals with respect to toleration: 'When nobody thinks for themselves there is no plurality of viewpoints to be heard and debated. Toleration then becomes pointless' (543).

There are two aspects of this process that merit closer consideration as they allow us to appreciate the political dynamic of this space. The first of these concerns the historicity of the 'public'. Although Kant's remarks about this term are confusing, what is clear is that this referent is constituted through argumentation or rhetoric. It does not correspond empirically or a priori to the terrain of the social. In fact, as Laursen (1986) has suggested, Kant's notion of the public was idiosyncratic by the standards of his contemporaries. In other words, it was not a public notion but rather one that Kant sought to publicize.[18] In this Kant exploited an ambivalence rooted in European jurisprudence between two senses of 'public'; the first referred to 'public' in the sense of 'out in the open', the second to the sense of 'public' as 'a matter of state'.[19] In so far as 'public' had been reduced to this second sense Kant reactivated the first in order to equate it with a sense of 'the people', or to name the people as such. Without question, this public was imagined through exclusion – for example, by its qualification as the 'entire reading public' which contradicts Kant's views on the 'entire fair sex'. Yet in the famous injunction to disagree in public and obey in private this exclusion takes place within the individual person. Although at first glance odd, this injunction is consistent with Kant's intervention. For Kant the form of private communication was derived from authority. It is only intelligible in terms of a specific aim that sustains a determined practice, as with a soldier or civil servant. Public speaking demonstrates through deed one's capacity to 'dare to think' and should be free from the direction of authority. The point is that this public enunciation is likely to have effects on one's private life. The distribution of appearances is upset such that no one remains in private where one thought oneself previously to be.[20]

This brings us to the second aspect. In publicizing reason Kant in effect privatizes authority, or confines it to a private sphere. Kant petitions authority to tolerate the process of reason and in doing this he conveniently provides reasons for authority to do so. Authority is legitimate if it supports enlightenment and to do this it has to be enlightened. Kant strives to reassure authority that no harm can come to it from this.[21] It has nothing to lose from doing so and everything to gain, not least an increase in esteem from those similarly enlightened. Lauded in this manner, who would not wish to be both enlightened and authoritative? This puts authority into dispute, which was arguably Kant's real purpose. In fact, Kant asserts that it is not authority but popular sentiments that constrain individuals to subjection. In part this can be construed as a further distancing of authority from an identity with the people, challenging the manner in which authority rests on the public.[22] Even revolutions can resort to prejudices which 'serve as a leash to control the great unthinking mass' (55).[23] Of course, little is said about authority tolerating those who Kant others. Yet Kant has undermined the means of enforcing any limit or border which would constrain such others to a proper place. Without rigid designation no one would know with confidence which side of this conflict they were on. Authority, such as it is, no longer knows whether in opposing revolution it undermines those popular sentiments on which it rests, and thus the capacity of the mass to be controlled and named. It is in this respect that Kant's thought is so corrosive. Kant's discourse is antagonistic in the course of accounting for antagonism.

There is no neutral enunciation in this space. Rather than inscribing a process that can be guaranteed, it is inscribed within a political causality that Kant destabilizes. Or rather, Kant establishes political causality as destabilization; does this political causality have a place in the structure of critique, either as an expression of the value of autonomy to be asserted or as the presence of heteronomy to be overcome? Does it concern an object that can be secured by transcendental conditions or is it merely empirical, unable to give an account of itself? Can it be reconciled with the noumenal self or is it merely phenomenal? In short, polemic becomes caught in the opposition between being completely determined, and thus not free, and being completely unconditioned, and thus otiose. In other words, why bother to argue? Kant does not address these questions directly. Instead, he poses something like a cause of political causality itself which does not have an ontotheological structure. The structure of this cause is paradoxical, aporetic. It is presented in another text published a month before the enlightenment essay where the argument hinges on the plausibility of free acts occurring behind the back of actors 'unconsciously promoting an end which, even if they knew what it was, would scarcely arouse their interest' (Kant 1991b [1784]). This end is enlightenment. The actors are without a plan of their own, indulging in 'childish malice and destructiveness' – hardly the actions of the 'entire reading public'. Such acts are teleological, cumulative, and natural. However, this does not by itself determine the necessity of their practical application. To do this Kant simply asserts the essentially antagonistic character of mankind. Thus:

> *The means which nature employs to bring about the development of innate capacities is that of antagonism within society, in so far as this antagonism becomes in the long run the cause of law-governed social order.* By antagonism, I mean in this context the *unsocial sociability* of men, that is, their tendency to come together in society, coupled, however, with a continual resistance which constantly threatens to break this society up. This propensity is obviously rooted in human nature. Man has an inclination to *live in society*, since he feels in this state more like a man, that is, he feels able to develop his natural capacities. But he also has a great tendency to *live as an individual*, to isolate himself, since he also encounters in himself the unsocial characteristic of wanting to direct everything in accordance with his own ideas. He therefore expects resistance all around, just as he knows of himself that he is in turn inclined to offer resistance to others. It is this very resistance which awakens all man's powers and induces him to overcome his tendency to laziness. Through the desire for honour, power or property, it drives him to seek status among his fellows, whom he cannot *bear* yet cannot *bear to leave*. (44)

Of course, this antagonistic quality is less than rational or empirical. It is an innovation within the tradition of modern political thought on the distinction between the natural and the social through that famous oxymoron 'human nature' which is renamed as the paradox that it is. In collapsing this distinction, Kant removes its *superstitious* character,[24] although its descriptive and impressionistic basis is retained. Everything contributes to transforming the '*pathologically* enforced social union' – necessity – into a '*moral* whole' – freedom (45).

For the first time conflict, antagonism, is recruited to philosophy as a positive good. 'All the culture and art which adorn mankind and the finest social order man creates are the fruits of his unsociability' (46). Not that these 'asocial qualities' are to be valued for their own sake, but only in so far as they enable man to avoid living a 'pastoral existence of perfect concord, self-sufficiency and mutual love' that denies the dignity of man. Indeed, the enclosure of freedom within 'a precinct like that of civil union' gives man's antagonistic nature the greatest effect as he strives to overcome these constraints, thus benefiting the whole species. The dignity of man is not to be himself in the present. In this case, as so often happens whenever the word is mentioned, nature is systematically ambivalent. It is as if nature has to be added to itself through a peculiar process whereby nature gives the gift of reason to man, which marks man's antagonistic nature as *asocial-social*, in order to receive it back modified as the realization of man's nature. The category of nature has been recruited to play a purely rhetorical role, a source of effects, which is itself empty of content except for a connotation of virtue and necessity beyond the scope of human interference.[25] Thus: 'Man wishes concord, but nature, knowing better what is good for his species, wishes discord' (45). Through this fabulous natural agency Man's nature, split between determination and self-determination, is prevented from being itself as, strictly speaking, this has yet to be determined. This means that for Kant nothing – man, reason, public, even others – can coincide with itself.[26] This coincidence is simply a matter of the indeterminate 'long run' that uses the superstition of providential nature against itself.

In this sense antagonism is the non-space of the political in Kant in that it is both ungrounded and ungrounding,[27] which is to say that freedom is interminable. It lives through a polemic that can never finally be resolved. Consequently, without the supplement of polemic pure reason cannot even be asserted as it prevents the suffocation of pure reason by dogma. Pure reason encourages conflict in so far as this undermines dogma, yet seeks to absent itself from it. It supports a generalized disconcertion from which it is immune only in so far as it affirms its own 'incompetence'. It does this by claiming to abstract itself with a concern with what is beyond the limits of what can be known, its horizon or boundary, although it has nothing positive to say about this. Polemic is only limited in that it cannot in itself decide with regard to the question of limits, of what can and cannot be known, and thus of what is beyond this. It can only demonstrate the contingency of things and not the necessity of that mode of reasoning through which such a demonstration occurs. This is the task of reason, but in carrying out this task it is supported by polemic. Polemic is the condition of critique through which pure reason is to be established and at the same time, in so far as this is supposed to be governed by the force of nature, it is its only positive effect. In this polemic cannot properly be anything. It calls into question established propriety precisely because it knows no boundaries. Here polemic is most critical precisely because it is contingent and ungrounded. Its metaphysical status is uncertain and provisional.

2.4 Polemicization and Metaphysics

The achievement and subsequent legacy of Kant's political thought has been read in various ways, although little attempt has been made to fold the historicity of Kant's thought back into it. For some Kant represents something like the self-consciousness of modernity expressed in logical form, as well as being symptomatic of the failure of modernity in terms of its impossible ambitions. Others, especially more recently, have been inspired by the analytical rigour of Kant's writing and have tried to imitate this as a guide for extending the ambitions of Kant's project in the direction of specifying the practical measures required for realizing the ethical arrangements it presented. Needless to say, this has been at the expense of the dimensions of historicity, critique and metaphysics. At the head of this group is John Rawls.

Rawls has claimed a relevance for his work by virtue of a Kantian lineage. If Schmitt and Kant can be used to show the failure of the opposition between philosophy and politics through which polemic emerges, albeit from opposite directions, then Rawls can be used to show the success of the identity between philosophy and politics. Polemic is absent because the identity of these terms is the point of departure for the argument. Rawls is so confident about this relation that it does not even need to be demonstrated. Yet this success entails that Rawls articulates the perspective of politics in the sense of police. In particular, our concern is with the alleged avoidance of metaphysics in Rawls's work. We argue that this is in fact a consequence of the constraints of his theory in which the empirical realm of politics, which for Rawls includes the tradition of modern political thought, is itself represented as metaphysical. For Rawls metaphysics has the status of common sense, such is the reliance of his argument on its unremarkable nature. Somewhat perversely, this avoidance has the effect of preventing what is publicized as its main advantage, the practical application of his theory on the basis of a moment's reflection. This is because ultimately Rawls is forced to recognize that the political world is not metaphysical enough. Rather than confront the consequences of this for his argument he takes refuge in the oldest of philosophical alibis, impotence.

Rawls has claimed that the relation between his thought and Kant's is one of 'analogy'. In this claim Kant is elevated to the level of an adjective (1980: 517). In *A Theory of Justice*, Rawls's Kantianism is based on the claim that the notion of the 'original position' that it elaborates prevents individuals from considering heteronomous or contingent elements in their deliberations on justice. This expressed their nature as autonomous, free, equal and rational beings. Thus: 'The description of the original position interprets the point of view of noumenal selves, of what it means to be a free and equal rational being' (1971: 255–6). The 'original position' locates the metaphysical status of freedom. It is the essence of freedom provided that the conditions in which it is expressed reflect it.[28] In turn freedom means the possibility of having a sense of justice although for Rawls being free is not a matter of justice or injustice. Freedom is understood as a fact which becomes relevant under certain conditions. For Rawls this means being deprived of knowledge of the contingencies of life through the 'veil of ignorance', a 'device of representation' designed to satisfy the liberal stipulation that justice is impartial but not neutral. More recently, Kant's 'categorical imperative' has been redescribed as a 'procedure' that determines the content of the moral law and which secures the autonomy of individuals as fact (1993: 292).

This lineage is condensed in another doctrine which Rawls derives from Kantian autonomy: namely, 'constructivism' (Rawls 1980). Rawls insists that this concept does not mean that persons and societies are made up. They exist factually as autonomous and self-grounding in so far as they are in accordance with their own natures as such, and which they can only do in so far as Rawls's procedure is accepted. If this is accepted, then morality itself has the status of fact. What gets constructed is the content of the 'categorical imperative,' which is at the same time the procedure for construction. The procedure itself is simply '*laid out*' (1993: 305, original emphasis). This is because not everything is constructed and anything which is constructed must be constructed out of something which preexists it. For Rawls what preexists construction is the principle of individuals as rational and autonomous. These moral facts or norms in turn determine other facts that are to count as relevant moral reasons

(1993: 308). Nothing needs to be added to the elements of the procedure as there are 'no independent criteria of justice; what is just is defined by the outcome of the procedure itself' (1980: 523). Justice is not 'perfect', but at least it is 'pure', to use Rawls's useful distinction, in the sense of true-to-itself, almost virginal.

In discussing Rawls we will critique the analogy that Rawls has proposed between his own theory and Kant's. This is because Rawls has no sense of the centrality of the critical-polemical dimension of antagonism that characterizes Kant's political project. Rawls wants to be friends with everyone. The analogy is not proportionate. In fact, Rawls's sense of the political is of the order of an established fact. Rather the reference to Kant is a strategic justification for his own theory of justice. The reason that Rawls relies on the contingent authority of a proper name has something to do with its ability to defend liberalism against criticisms which liberals might come up with. One recalls that the last section of A Theory of Justice was concerned with 'justification'. This is a matter of 'everything fitting together into one coherent view' (1971: 579). It is 'addressed to those who disagree with us, or to ourselves when we are of two minds' (580). In its reliance on reason and the law of contradiction it is Socratic in method and proceeds from the assumption of consensus in which reason is located. The content of this consensus is not arbitrary, as Rawls claims that it comprehends 'the leading traditional theories' and amounts to a defence of the contractarian tradition and thus of that society which Rawls claims is founded on contract (581). For Rawls the name of Kant hegemonizes this tradition in so far as it deemphasizes utilitarianism and economism, the main rivals in determining the tone and conduct of moral philosophy. At the same time Kant's name gives this tradition an empirical purchase over which utilitarianism and economism had previously enjoyed exclusivity.

A Theory of Justice poses the question of justice because it takes as its point of intervention the claim that individuals are split between exercising 'the capacity for an effective sense of justice' and the capacity to pursue an individual conception of the good. Rawls grounds this distinction empirically through recourse to the distinction between the reasonable and the rational – or, in terms of 'the tradition', between civic duty and individual freedom.[29] Through the 'categorical imperative procedure' one rationally decides to be reasonable. This means accepting the conditions that have allowed one to act rationally, pursuing individual interests or conceptions of the good, on the assumption that they will continue to support one's endeavour in this way. Individual reason is reconciled with social reasonableness on the terrain of distributive justice. The practical outcome is the reconciliation of individuals to the basic structure of society. In achieving this, freedom and equality become expressions of this structure, and the political is reduced to this relation. The objectivity of justice, which Rawls derives from his notion of 'constructivism', is given by its authority and must be recognized by all those subject to it (1980: 554). Objectivity is not 'true' but 'reasonable'. It is the basis of social cooperation which those subject to it must adhere to, as they are deemed to hold it as 'common sense'. In this case the logic of identity is prescriptive. As Rawls points out in his reply to Habermas (1995), this is not a matter of voting.[30] It is 'founded on reasonable beliefs as established by society's generally accepted methods of inquiry' (1980: 521). Rawls insists that such a society has no need of ideology. It is a transparent society, by which quality 'publicity' itself is defined (1980: 539).

We would argue, following Rancière, that this relies on an absolute coincidence between philosophy and politics. To demonstrate this we will refer to Rawls's own arguments that claim that his theory does not require any philosophical dimension at all, although as far as we know this has not caused Rawls to renounce its alleged Kantian dimension. These arguments were posed defensively in response to a series of challenges, beginning with Sandel (1982), that stressed the priority of the local, contingent and particular and which advocated the ethical sufficiency of these forms of existence and various political projects that would secure them. This advocacy is commonly known as *communitarianism*.[31] At the same time these elements were found to be equally present in Rawls's theory but were disguised by a vocabulary and style which suggested that the relevance of the theory was universal. Rawls was accused of presupposing an 'unencumbered' notion of the self that was impossible to sustain against the primacy of the 'situated self', and of arguing that justice should be derived from a procedure blind to particulars as a means to advance a conception of justice that was itself particular. To varying degrees these challenges implied that Rawls's account was only relevant to a specific political regime, that of North American liberal democracy, and thus contrary to its central claim elevated a substantive notion of the good over a formal notion of right. In other words, Rawls passed off the particular as the universal. In this Rawls was simply trying to be hegemonic.

Rawls's subsequent work has been concerned to negotiate the impact of these challenges while at the same time preserving and advancing the basic aim of *A Theory of Justice*.[32] This has been done by insisting that the theory has no need of any metaphysical or 'comprehensive view'. Instead it should be properly understood as a political theory of justice, although what is meant by political is ambiguous. Rawls admits that it could simply mean 'moral'. In any event, for Rawls it doesn't mean much more than the fact that the theory 'starts from within a certain political tradition' and addresses certain basic intuitive ideas 'embedded in the political institutions of a constitutional democratic regime and the public traditions of their interpretation' (1985: 225).[33] This has lead Honig to suggest that Rawls has moved a lot closer to his communitarian and substantive critics (1993: 195). If this is the case, then it is not difficult to see why. It is no accident that in confronting their criticisms Rawls has found it remarkably easy to deemphasize any elements of his work that could be considered metaphysical. In other words, who needs metaphysics if reality is like that anyway? As Honig has claimed in a more critical vein on the basis of Sandel's criticism, 'Rawls's language of choice is a decoy; acknowledgement is the deep truth of the original position', which gives rise to the 'always-already being repeated' of the 'original position' (1993: 136). In this scenario heteronomous facts are at the service of a noumenal self which simply mirrors them. Consequently, the advantage of accepting the communitarian critique is that it offers Rawls the empirical grounding in the particularity of a tradition that his theory requires if it is to enjoy any sort of authority. That is to say, these critics achieved the work of empirical verification which Rawls's theory presupposed but did not demonstrate.

It is because of this that we reject the main thrust of the communitarian criticism of Rawls, as it is limited by a fantasy which it shares with Rawls himself: namely, that societies exist and are sufficient to themselves and self-contained. This fantasy is sustained by the metaphysical conviction that an object – whether a modern liberal society or anti-modern traditional community – can be described exhaustively and that the description corresponds to its object. This objection is supported by Hardt and Negri's summary of the impossibility of Rawls's theory, which is derived from Ricœur's criticisms (1988, 1990). *A Theory of Justice* 'rests on a circular form of exposition in which the argument's point of departure and its conclusion presuppose one another' such that 'the argument must be finished before it can properly begin' (1994: 229). This circularity is embedded within Rawls's description of a 'well-ordered society', the status of which is that it is 'freestanding' in that it recognizes nothing which would undermine its representation of its own self-sufficiency, and which defines its constructed nature or its experience of objectivity. Thus:

> To continue: recall that a well-ordered society is conceived as an on-going society, a self-sufficient association of human beings which, like a nation-state, controls a connected territory. Its members view their common polity as extending backward and forward in time over generations, and they strive to reproduce themselves, and their cultural and social life in perpetuity, practically speaking: that is, they would envisage any final date at which they were to wind up their affairs as inadmissible and foreign to their conception of their association. Finally, a well-ordered society is a closed system; there are no significant relations to other societies, and no one enters from without, for all are born into and lead a complete life. (1980: 536)

The simultaneity of the beginning and ending of a closed and homogeneous self-reproducing spatio-temporal system is the basic social dynamic. Society is itself the subject which determines the distribution of the individuals who comprise it as its expression. It is *autopoietic*, to borrow the alibi of 'systems theory'. In this, society is reduced to the crudest myth of a tradition. Both society and tradition are self-identical and the source of all problems to which they themselves provide the solution, an ideological representation in the critical Marxist sense. In fact, one could say that ontotheology is reinscribed or institutionalized within a sociological description of a perfect society as a 'sociological utopia' which would dispense with both philosophy and politics through presuming their coincidence.[34] Rawls's claim to have withdrawn from metaphysics is in fact a device by which metaphysics coincides with the political understood as the empirical but no less metaphysical space of politics.

The name of this device is 'the method of avoidance' (1985: 231). For Rawls, this method is the only way in which justice will work, and which arises from the manner in which Rawls conceives the occasion for justice. Within Rawls's social description a 'fundamental social fact' is recognized which liberals normally understand as pluralism. This fact is the assumption that in a constitutional democratic state under modern conditions there are bound to exist 'conflicting and incommensurable conceptions of the good. This feature characterizes modern culture since the Reformation' (245). The existence of 'value pluralism' is simply proof of the fact of equality. Yet as all are equal none can provide the means to settle the disputes which Rawls believes arise from this plurality. To deal with this Rawls seeks to establish an 'overlapping consensus', which is imagined as an appeal to 'intuitive' reasonableness through which 'citizens' agree to avoid disputed philosophical, moral and religious questions because these cannot be resolved politically. Social cooperation is thus built upon mutual respect for differences. According to Hampton, this device is simply a *modus vivendi* in which toleration is instrumental and expedient (1989). In other words, it does not matter whether individuals actually agree with liberalism and pluralism. All that matters is that they are prepared to appear to agree with liberalism and pluralism because it is in their interests to do so. Yet this criticism is misplaced in that it too verifies Rawls's description. It accepts as fact the existence of a plurality of antagonistic metaphysical views understood as discrete and incommensurable entities.[35] It also accepts that pluralism is 'political not metaphysical'. Against this we would argue that for Rawls plurality constitutes the plenitude of the political. It is a metaphysical plenitude of mathematical equality in which each discrete entity corresponds to one. This metaphysics inscribes a purely political decision that trumps each and any particularity because it is what each and any particularity presupposes: that is, that they exist as one in a world characterized by the existence of other ones. This is true even in such cases when such ones seek to eliminate other ones or when they do not rate their individuality or freedom as highly as other forms of belonging which they prefer to be subject to. In this sense liberalism is hegemonic.[36] Through this Rawls elevates and exaggerates the role of incommensurable metaphysical views as a cause of conflict precisely in order to allow a space for a political decision that inscribes a limit on the basis of a metaphysical pluralism.

So, instead of eliminating metaphysics, this method is a means with which to avoid the test of the validity of the description.[37] In this Rawls is as far from Kant as possible. Kant's formula is simply reversed. One is to agree in public but disagree in private. At the same time, the public itself has become privatized. It is simply another private zone that happens to be the one through which power over all other private zones is to be exercised. Yet Rawls also undermines the validity of his own description, or rather reveal its limits. This is the admission that the 'well-ordered society' does not exist by virtue of the presence of 'dispute' within it:

> Our society is not well-ordered: the public conception of justice and its understanding of freedom and equality are in dispute. Therefore, for us – you and me – a basis of public justification is still to be achieved. (1980: 569)

Although Rawls's strategy is to bring this into being by basing it on what 'we' know already, at the end of the day even 'we' may not possess a 'reasonable and workable conception of justice'. In which case, 'This would mean that the practical task of political philosophy is doomed to failure (570)', that is, in addressing 'common sense', political philosophy finds that its response is 'hesitant' and 'uncertain' and 'doesn't know what to think'. Under these circumstances Rawls feels that political philosophy can legitimately 'propose to it certain conceptions and principles congenial to its most essential convictions and historical traditions' (518). In other words, that task of philosophy is simply to remind society of its essential identity. Yet Rawls also specifies the typical occasions on which one may apply his doctrine. These are when society is characterized by fundamental and divisive 'political controversy' (1985: 226). At all costs it is the basis of this controversy that cannot be remembered. This is the non-identity of society with its representation or with metaphysics. So, for Rawls it is what we are supposed to know already that will test us. In this Rawls is essentially Platonic. Yet the dimension of contingency and historicity was unknown to Plato in the ways that it is known to modernity. Thus Rawls relies on a certain selectivity in what we know already, of which the 'veil of ignorance' is merely the symptom. This selectivity is determined by the political distribution of appearances. Rawls provides an alibi for this determination by affirming the impotence of his theory. This is the basis for the *entre nous* of community.

2.5 Polemicization and Plurality

Finally, in order to broaden the discussion, we will consider some attempts that have tried to wrestle with the persistence of the relationship between philosophy and politics without relying on the collapse of each term into the other through recourse to the assumption of the One. This persistence is not a matter of their identity but of their errancy. Ultimately, this reduces to the unavoidable challenge of thinking the political – that is to say, of those dimensions of conflict that cannot be reconciled with the metaphysical certainties of philosophy or the empirical certainties of politics. In this we seek to extend the democratic imaginary described in the first chapter in so far as this dimension of conflict dislocates the distribution of appearances.

Let us consider the matter in these terms. Is it possible to accept the fact of pluralism as Rawls wishes to do and at the same time allow for the possibility of the contestation of the distribution of appearances, or must one in fact situate the fact of pluralism within the distribution of appearances itself as a concern of the police in Rancière's sense? This would seem to have been the fate of so-called 'multiculturalism'. If one wishes to avoid subscribing to the platitudes of liberalism, as Rawls expresses and systematizes them, then it would be hard to avoid the second option. However, this option comes at an enormous cost. It requires that one identifies, if not actually occupies, a position exterior to the distribution of appearances. Kant tried this with the notion of critique but this relied on a polemical engagement within appearances, or its copresence with appearances, such that an exterior transcendental realm could never finally be established. Thus the real difficulty that determines the cost of exteriority is not isolation from the comforts of the familiar but rather the impossibility of demonstrating that such an exterior position is identifiable, or could ever be reached. That is to say, the only proof that one would have of reaching this state would be the fact that there would be no one around to confirm it. In this light, perhaps it is more fruitful to return to the theme of the contestation of the distribution of appearances from Rancière's 'nonplace as place', as this undermines the appearance of the distinction between an interior and an exterior that satisfies the police. After all, one would not wish to do the job of verifying this distinction for them.

Here we can reconsider the distinction between philosophy and politics itself. Rawls's underlying metaphysical commitment receives its expression in the principle of unanimity from which legitimacy derives. This principle comprehends difference and diversity in so far as each differential element is understood as or counts for one. Thus: 'The original position is so characterized that unanimity is possible; the deliberations of any one person are typical of all' in so far as everyone 'has a similar sense of justice and in this respect a well-ordered society is homogeneous. Political argument appeals to this moral consensus' (1971: 263). Each element is thus equal with each and every other element in the form of a moral consensus – thus raising the issue of how dispute actually arises, and of why Rawls cannot ultimately eliminate it. Yet despite Rawls's intention to institute the flattest distribution of difference as possible, geometrical distribution remains over which procedural justice lacks jurisdiction. This is not to say that geometrical distribution is stable, a rock-solid social fact in the face of which justice is impotent. Rather, it is the dynamic of its distribution which is undetermined by justice. Justice has no interest in eliminating the forces of inequality, the concealments of power that authorize the distribution of appearances.

Consequently, in practical terms unanimity is always expressed as something less than itself: that is, as majority. Unanimity simply remains as the *telos* of legitimacy in a less than perfect world.

In his critique of Rawls's notion of deliberation, the procedure through which justice is decided, Manin accepts Rawls's claim that the value of unanimity can be traced back to Rousseau's concept of the 'General Will' in so far as it too imagines the participation of individuals in the decision through which community is unified around its sense of justice (Manin 1987).[38] This lineage is the initial target of Manin's intervention in which the decision is a moment present to itself in which all participate on the basis of mutual indifference. Manin points out that on this basis deliberation is not in fact what it claims to be in being a decision. In Rousseau deliberation is absent, or rather, it is used as 'decision' instead of the usual sense of 'the process of formation of the will, the particular moment that precedes choice, and in which the individual ponders different solutions before settling for one of them' (Manin 1987: 345). Unanimity assumes that the subject possesses a fully self-determining will that is simply registered or represented in an act of agreement with others. This act is spontaneous and the will of individuals is formed prior to it such that 'The process of forming a decision is reduced to calculation' (Manin 1987: 349). Political rationality is substituted by an idealized economic rationality. Against this account Manin argues that political deliberation is in fact more accurately characterized as 'choice under uncertainty'. Politics proceeds both from the recognition that society is not 'well-ordered' and the recognition that this is not cause for despair but optimism. Thus, against Rawls and Rawls's version of the contractarian tradition Manin removes legitimacy from its foundation in the predetermined will of individuals and relocates it 'in the process of its formation, that is, deliberation itself' (352). It is not a decision but a process of becoming informed about decisions in which the nature of the individual will is constantly transformed in the absence of any final or total state of affairs. This is because the will and the individuals who embody it cannot be fully determined either autonomously or heteronomously. Means and ends are radically indeterminate. Preferences remain incomplete and incoherent and give rise to multiple forms of conflict with others. Importantly, that which is plural is always in a process of formation, always more or less than one.

The process of deliberation is understood in terms of argumentation that does not presuppose consensus but seeks to build it. In common with Perelman and Olbrechts-Tyteca (1969) and others, rhetoric is given priority over the self-image of science in political discourse. This process requires a multiplicity of perspectives and openness to these that is secured by a commitment to the legitimacy of the process and not necessarily the outcome. That one is open does not entail that one agrees. No outcome is ever final and is always contingent. In fact, plurality is the condition of argumentation and thus legitimacy because it raises the issue of justification. On this account pluralism does not require an assumption of optimal equilibrium. Of course, this is unbalanced in favour of majorities precisely because these are never the unanimity of the one that comprehends all. Moreover, argumentation is always relative to an audience. Manin does not say much about the nature of this audience or the actual practice of deliberation but he does describe the process of deliberation. This is characterized as 'a sort of competition for generality. The deliberative process never results in strictly universal proposals; universality remains the unattainable end, but the system provides an *incentive to generalization*' (359, original emphasis). Deliberation is never finally hegemonic but has a tendency to become so, which only reaches a general level and which preserves other alternatives for becoming hegemonic in its ability to render them implausible but not necessarily wrong. Majorities and minorities are continually recomposed. Importantly, 'Although the decision does not conform to all points of view, it is the result of the confrontation between them' (359). Legitimacy arises from the fact of confrontation and not from the arbitrarily assigned point at which deliberation ends and a decision is taken.

Manin's argument, which obliquely refers to elected parliamentary democracies as exemplary, corrects Rawls's account of the legitimacy of pluralism. Importantly, in addition to defending argumentation it also defends individual liberty and freedom against its communitarian critics who try to bypass this problem through appeals to 'the pathos of "community" and its unfathomable mystery' (351) into which Rawls ultimately fell. No one would wish to abandon the achievement of the modern individual yet equally this achievement is undermined if individuality is itself communalized – that is to say, if individuality is reduced to being a function of a *system* or if individuality is identical with itself and self-contained. Manin's reliance on the accomplishment of pluralism risks doing exactly this such that each is a one equivalent to every other one in so far as each one participates in argumentation. This participation sometimes looks like a passive matter of accepting or rejecting propositions but not their active formation, in the same way that Rawls imagined the intervention of philosophy into a 'common sense' which is doomed to reject it – that is, describing plurality from the point of view of the ideal outcome, pluralist competition. The dimension of incompletion and incoherence is denied any ontological dignity. Given that this constitutes the motor of deliberation this is surprising. It overlooks those entities that are more or less than one in so far as they do not occupy a predetermined place in the geometry of the *system*, and thus a position of enunciation from which to argue – Rancière's *proletarii*. These are not functional. At the same time, Manin recognizes this characteristic as the indeterminacy of the will while remaining ambivalent about the cause of its determination. This determination could simply be a characteristic of the *system*. Therefore, the nature of this indeterminacy needs to be deepened in order to reveal its polemicizing character, or the difference of the *system* from itself – that is, a pluralism that is never one.

Connolly's notion of the 'ontopolitical' does exactly this through reinscribing metaphysics within the plural space of antagonism (1995). On the one hand, this is by bringing a plurality of metaphysical views back into the social space from which Rawls had excluded them through acknowledging their incommensurability as grounds for an ethos of agonistic respect for differences. This may be open to the charge that a plurality of metaphysical views was never there in the first place to any significant political degree, or that the political efficacy of metaphysical views is exaggerated, which would reduce Connolly to a reversal of Rawls. On the other hand, in reality Connolly is in fact simply pointing out that other approaches to politics are not exterior to metaphysics, especially if they deny their own metaphysical dimension. This does not demonstrate that the plurality of different approaches to politics corresponds to an equivalent plurality of metaphysical assumption and that these are the basis of their conflict. More interestingly, Connolly identifies the metaphysics underlying such a plurality in terms of the ontological status of becoming, or, more accurately, in terms of a conflict between being and becoming that Connolly translates into a political conflict between fundamentalism and democracy. Fundamentalism corresponds to the refusal to acknowledge the contingency of one's position and the violent assertion of one's right to protect this refusal. Democracy is the opposite of this, which enters into antagonistic relations because it aims to expose contingency through asserting its own 'ontopolitical interpretation' of the priority of contingency against fundamentalism's refusal to do so. Although Connolly does not put it in these terms, democracy is a form of violence.

What makes Connolly's position important is that fundamentalism is not confined to some imaginary space external to enlightened modernity but is located within it, which amounts to the assertion that there is no space exterior to modernity and that modernity is not a self-contained substance. Moreover, the opposition between fundamentalism and democracy is not something exterior to modernity. It is something that has happened through modernity. Connolly summarizes this as 'the globalization of contingency' (22). This is contextualized empirically by the emergence of a post-Marxist emphasis on civil society, globalization and population displacement, the general speeding up of communication and transformation, the emergence of claims for 'positive identities' amongst formerly marginalized social groups, and the collapse of the differences between individualism and communitarianism (1995: xi). In this context pluralism is itself fundamentalism in that it imagines that those differences that it takes to be plural are in fact stable self-contained entities, a plurality of ones subsumed under the one of pluralism. Pluralism as fundamentalism refuses to acknowledge its own contingency and the becoming contingent of itself as the dynamic through which it is produced. It is incapable of acknowledging its own disidentification from itself, the ontological dimension of incoherency and incompletion through which it becomes something other. Connolly calls this disidentification *pluralization*. It gives rise to a conflict between entities that imagine themselves to be essential and the movement of those entities which we would characterize as more or less than one which exist through their own contingency and which are produced by the efforts of preexisting pluralism to maintain its own identity. Connolly describes the dynamic of this antagonism in the following terms:

> at its most fragile point a new possibility of being both disrupts the stability of established identities and lacks a sufficiently stable definition through which to present itself. This is because to *become* something new is to *move* the self-recognition and relational standards of judgement endorsed by other constituencies to whom you are connected. (xvi)

This violent movement of displacement is reflective, preventing the sedimentation of movement into identity through a 'politics of disturbance'.

Connolly is concerned to formulate an ethical comportment within this politics of disturbance that acknowledges contingency and yet at the same time affirms the dimension of attachment that contingency disturbs. The object of this attachment is democracy-as-becoming. Connolly calls this ethical comportment a 'critical responsiveness' that 'draws sustenance from an almost always operative attachment to life as a protean set of energies and possibilities exceeding the terms of any identity or cultural horizon into which it is set' (28). In practice this amounts to an identification with vitality as the force of becoming. This is a difficult position to occupy, which is exactly the point. It is not an identity. In so far as one would equate action and existence then such an ethics can only be provisional and voluntary, as pluralization demonstrates that no such equation is reliable. In fact, Connolly acknowledges as much when he observes that 'The most persistent issue facing critical interpretation today is the ironic relation it assumes to its own ontopolitical projections' (38). This would include the privilege of becoming over being itself. In fact, it may be that a way beyond this irony, which has become commonplace, is to give up on the attachment to being or becoming, or the belief that ontology grounds identification. Rather, ontology prevents the fullness of subjectivity in which a traditional ethical relation is possible. Critique and dogma continue antagonistically. In this, subjectivity is more a matter of the suddenness of wit, of the unexpected flash through which the heterogeneous is combined in fragments.[39] In the following chapter we situate this experience of subjectivity.

Notes

1. Neither Rancière nor ourselves understand political philosophy as 'academic commentaries on a few canonical authors or grand declarations that politics has come to an end' (1995a: 171). Sadly, this is what it has become. Elsewhere, in discussing the alleged revival of political philosophy, Rancière states that:

   > the main aim seems to be to ensure communication between the great classic doctrines and the usual forms of state legitimization that we know as liberal democracies. But the supposed convergence between the return of political philosophy and the return of its object, politics, is lacking in evidence. (1998: viii)

2. For an account of the various uses of Nietzsche, see Larmore (1996). For a critical overview of recent literature that desires to set up a relation between 'The New Nietzsche' and the political within the traditional relation between philosophy and politics, see Coole (1998).

3. This judgement probably owes more to Heidegger and Derrida than Descombes would like to admit.
4. In this we would support the aim of thinking 'with Nietzsche against Nietzsche' (Ferry and Renaut 1997: vii).
5. As Nietzsche himself once put it,

> truths are illusions of which one has forgotten that they *are* illusions; worn out metaphors which have become powerless to affect the senses; coins which have their obverse effaced and now are no longer of account as coins but merely as metal. (1911 [1873]: 180)

   It would be a shame if Nietzsche suffered a similar fate, although there are no compelling reasons to prevent this from happening.
6. The first aspect illustrates the Derridian theme of the 'constitutive outside', as outlined by Staten (1984: 15–19). The double status of the limit bears a family resemblance to the distinction between dislocation and antagonism advanced by Laclau (1990: 39–40).
7. In this our approach coincides with Derrida (1997).
8. Skinner (1996) gives numerous examples of the development of this figure from Aristotle to Hobbes.
9. Derrida suggests that Schmitt's insistence on the paradoxical notion of 'real possibility' as the ultimate ground of the distinction between friend/enemy as it posits the annihilation of each is 'a rhetorical ploy in a disguised polemic' (126).
10. As Derrida points out, 'it is no easy task to decide whether this decision supposes, rends, undermines or produces the community; or to decide what binds it to itself in a friendly attraction or self-conservation which resembles *philía* or *philautía*' (1997: 126). Moreover, as 'exceptionality grounds the eventuality of the event', it acquires a simultaneously predictable and impossible character such that: 'An event is an event, and a decisive one, only if it is exceptional. An event as such is always exceptional' (128). As Frye (1966) pointed out, if the political is to be linked with the exception, then it only applies to the domestic scene, as war between nation states is a common condition in the absence of an authority to decide war between nation states.
11. For an even more interesting approach to the problem of the decision in Schmitt, see Weber (1992).
12. 'Schmitt does not so much define the political by oppositional negation as define the latter by the political. This inversion stems from a teleological law of power or intensity' (Derrida 1997: 139).

13. Derrida refers to Schmitt's later *The Theory of the Partisan* as a text through which Schmitt began to grasp the implications of this, and thus presumably the political character of modernity. For Derrida this character is 'the spectre, lodged within the political itself; the antithesis of the political dwells within, and politicizes, the political' (138). Yet it seems that right to the end Schmitt could not grasp 'the fact that telluric autochtony is *already a reactive response to a delocalization and to a form of tele-technology*, whatever its degree of elaboration, its power, or its speed' (142).

14. The concept of every rational being as one who must regard himself as making universal law by all the maxims of his will, and must seek to judge himself and his actions from this point of view, leads to a closely connected and very fruitful concept – namely, that of *a kingdom of ends.* (Kant 1989: 95)

15. More precisely, in part II, 'The Transcendental Doctrine of Method', Chapter 1, 'The Discipline of Pure Reason', section 2, 'The Discipline of Pure Reason in Respect of its Polemical Employment'.

16. Kant argues that the 'concept of an absolutely necessary being' is a concept of pure reason. Instead of attempting to prove the existence of this entity, Kant is concerned with the conditions which make it necessary 'in order that we may determine whether or not, in resorting to this concept, we are thinking anything at all'. To insist that this being is 'unconditioned', or 'is', simply repeats the problem, as does the argument that existence is a predicate of the concept. Tactically, however, Kant leaves the issue undecided in the sense that he only shows that the grounds for asserting the existence of such a being are unfounded. This does not prove that such a being does not exist.

17. This dimension of enlightenment still has the power to disconcert. Stanley Rosen has found himself astonished by this 'invention on a global scale of the rhetoric of frankness', which he demonizes by making it license postmodernism (Rosen 1987: 27). Rosen's main objection to Kant is that 'critique is both judge and jury' because it is 'not independent of the free use of reason' (36). Thankfully, Rosen offers no advice as to how one would reinstitute propriety.

18. In making this point Laursen seeks to correct the view that Kant was 'a timid philosopher who never dared to defy the political authorities' (584).

19. Bobbio (1989, especially Chapter 1) outlines the various senses of 'public' in European thought.

20. In our view, the popular feminist slogan 'the personal is political' is an extension of Kant's subversion of the private/public distinction.

21. In this we agree with Dolar's identification of the political dimension of Kant's philosophy or

> a political dimension in the theoretical as such – it is a space which is itself devoid of power, but which sets the limits to every form of power and thus makes apparent the element of arbitrariness, or contingency, implied within it. The renunciation of power is the source of the power of philosophy; its powerless appeal is its strongest weapon. Its appeal is always I have no power over you, but this is what makes it invincible. The law which commands, prohibits and threatens appears powerless compared to this weak voice. (1995: 272)

This is not to underestimate the disavowal of this powerlessness.

22. Kant was adept at the negotiation of these contingencies. After the succession of Frederick William III, one of the more notorious 'mad kings of Europe' who increased press censorship, Kant restricted the scope of disagreement to university professors who could do no harm because of their impotence. This forms the context of Kant's later essay 'The Contest of the Faculties' (1798). Again, Kant was dissembling, although this could not be said of his twentieth-century imitators in the so-called 'analytic' tradition who resemble Kant's theologians in endlessly determining what cannot be said.

23. For us this evokes one of the great lines of Beckett's prose: 'habit is the leash which ties the dog to its vomit.'

24. An example of this is provided by Locke who, recognizing the insufficiency of the law of nature, explains conflict in terms of the accident of corruption. Thus:

> And were it not for the corruption and vitiousness of degenerate Men, there would be no need of any other; no necessity that Men should separate from this great and natural Community, and by positive agreements combine into smaller and divided associations. (1991 [1679–82 (disputed)]: 352)

25. For an important discussion of the ambivalent role of nature in Kant's attempt to secure freedom, see Derrida (1981).

26. Dolar points out that in this failure of subjectivity Kant was more radical than Foucault's reservations suggest in that Kant launches modern subjectivity as an ethic of self-creation. 'The subject of the

Enlightenment, for Kant, is a split subject and can only remain free as long as it accepts this split. The persistent split is the place of freedom, not something to be overcome' (1995: 268). Following Lacan, Dolar refers to the impossibility of full subjectivity as 'the subject'. Our reservations about this approach are discussed in the following chapter. For a further discussion of the Foucault/Kant issue that aims to affirm the limits of self-creation, see Venn (1997).

27. In this conclusion we would hope to have overcome the antinomy arrived at by Howard (1989) in attempting to provide a Kantian account of the political. This asserts that the political should be seen as the conditions of possibility of political life while at the same time arguing that this is impossible. Our argument is that this is constitutive. Howard's book remains instructive in presenting the aporias of the political.

28. Honig and Kelly's criticism of Kant would easily apply to Rawls.

29. As Mouffe points out, 'reasonable' means nothing more than persons who 'accept the fundamentals of liberalism', thus substituting a political decision for a moral exigency (Mouffe 1995: 1538). However, this decision may not be as exclusionary as Mouffe suggests, given that Rawls is reluctant to give it any more content than a recognition of social cooperation. It is a more or less 'empty signifier', hence its hegemonic appeal.

30. 'The conception of political justice can no more be voted on than can the axioms, principles and rules of inference of mathematics or logic' (Rawls 1995: 144).

31. For an account of the opposition between 'liberal and communitarians' on Rawls's behalf, see Mulhall and Swift (1992). For a critical engagement with the debate that usefully distinguishes between ontological and advocacy issues, see Taylor (1989).

32. Much of this is condensed in Rawls (1993).

33. For a powerful critique of Rawls's notion of the political from a position sympathetic to Schmitt, see Mouffe (1993). Mouffe argues that Rawls's disavowal of the political condemns liberalism to 'perpetual irrelevance' (1995: 1543). We would argue that this irrelevance is not without effects.

34. According to Yack's penetrating criticism, 'Rawls miraculously rediscovers philosophic conceptions in nonphilosophic practices' (1993: 234).

35. At least Hampton has the courage of her convictions in that she is prepared to argue against such views if they are wrong.

36. Yack suggests that the claim that liberals 'avoid imposing their conceptions on others contributes to the popularity of their theories' (1993: 235).

37. Yack's observations on this point are worth quoting: 'One begins to wonder whether Rawls has not simply replaced an unrealistic conception of human nature with an equally unrealistic conception of democratic "public culture" ' by simply writing 'his conception of moral personality into democratic public culture' rather than discovering it (1993: 232). As Yack points out, few Americans would separate desert and justice in the way that Rawls thinks they do. One wonders if Rawls has ever read a newspaper or watched Jerry Springer.

38. Indeed, for Rawls Kant simply gave a 'philosophical foundation' to this concept from which Rawls removes, or claims to remove, 'its metaphysical surroundings' (Rawls 1971: 264).

39. Here we refer to Critchley's discussion of the relation between wit and irony in Romanticism (1997).

Chapter 3

Polemicizing Subjectivity

3.1 The Modern Subject

A common preoccupation of theoretical discussion in the human sciences since at least the mid-1970s has been with the question of the political dimension of the subject. In many respects this can be understood as the continuation of the modern dilemma of free will and determinism by other means. This continuation coheres around the question of how social and political agency is to be understood in its determination and constitution, or the extent to which agency is self-constituting and determining. If agency is posed in this way, to explain it in terms of the self, or autonomy, or the category of the same, is at the same time to attribute an ethical value to agency, or at least to secure its dignity. The advantage of the notion of the subject is that it allows for a degree of exteriority towards these sorts of question such that they can still be posed but in a manner that does not necessarily reproduce their underlying assumptions, and thus confirm the coincidence of explanation and ethical value. This critical distance leaves open the question of the 'who' or the 'what' of the subject and at the same time allows for a greater sensitivity to material questions of location and determination, and above all of the relation of the subject to power. Consequently, the political is located within the question of the subject itself, displacing its taken-for-granted status. Unfortunately, the notion of the subject admits of at least three distinct meanings, all of which are associated with claims regarding their political significance. Pointing out this fact should not be taken as a reason for dismissing the pertinence of the term, or to announce an intention to clarify the concept. It is simply to mark the natural tendency to conflate these different meanings under the constraints of linguistic economy. Nevertheless, this conflation is not unmotivated. The relation between these three meanings is not without order, hierarchy or rank, and this is a matter of consequence for the manner in which the political subject is discussed. Here we wish to intervene in this hierarchy, to polemicize this ordering, rather than reduce the subject to a univocal point. This is because all three meanings have their uses.

Perhaps the most familiar and flexible meaning of the subject is the grammatical one, as in the subject of a sentence, and thus of a text or discourse. Here it means that which the action is about or determined by. It could be a person or any other agent to which action is attributed, such as a nation, a football team or even the wind. On this basis it also refers to the 'speaking subject', the position of enunciation or intelligibility implied by the location of the grammatical subject, and much work has been concerned with demonstrating that these two moments can never coincide, or with the affirmation of the 'split' subject of discourse. As is well known, this development has drawn on structural linguistics, semiotics and Lacanian psychoanalysis. The force of this approach derives from its use in disclosing that subjects are never who they imagine themselves to be. More recently, this grammatical sense has been given a less critical inflection in order to protect the dignity of the imaginary dimension of the subject, to support the identification between the subject and subjectivity. To this end the subject is understood as no more or less than radically situated, with the effect that there are as many subjects as there can be said to be discourses that constitute them. The purpose of this is to mark a resistance to the subsumption of these subjects under one over-arching discourse, which is commonly known as a 'politics of identity' or a 'politics of difference'. This is a strategy for affirming the dignity of particular, often marginalized, situations and the subjects that occupy them. In this instance one refers to a particular subject-position under the heading of the situation or discourse in which the subject occurs. The subject is constrained to be a subject of a particular type, although this places a great deal of faith in the capacity of subjects to occupy the enunciation through which these discourses are enunciated, even if these discourses are locally produced. It requires a strategic amnesia with respect to the critical lessons of semiotics and psychoanalysis. It is simply cynical and intellectually dishonest to try and justify this disavowal as a justifiable compensation for marginalization and the experience of being dominated.[1]

In addition it is often claimed that doing this automatically constitutes a political effect through which the ethical categories of difference or identity are upheld. Claims of this sort may well be verified on some occasions. After all, who would wish to live in a world of dull uniformity as opposed to endless variety? Yet this tells us nothing about how such a situation is, or indeed becomes, political, except in so far as it upholds the values of pluralism. In fact, the opposite is equally possible in that the affirmation of particularity can, and often does, have the perverse effect of deriving the dignity of the subject from its determined or constrained nature. Here the political value of the subject is simply a function of the reproduction of the situation that sustains it. In so far as such situations are produced through inequality, then this inequality becomes internalized as the positive expression of the dignity of the subject, rather than becoming an opening for what Rancière refers to as *'subjectivization'*. Not surprisingly, this gives rise to some rather curious pathologies of *ressentiment*. Although it is often claimed that this political value can be redeemed as the self-determination of the subject, in practice this is impossible to demonstrate as there is no original situation that one could point to that is not differentially determined through uneven relations of power. No authentic subject is available that would function as a ground, although it is a notable empirical characteristic of these situations that a sort of ventriloquism emerges to authorize authenticity. The absence of a ground encourages rival ventriloquisms and the process in which the matter gets sorted out can be extremely disagreeable, which is perhaps what is really meant by a 'politics of difference'. In fact, the paradox of the assertion of the principle of particularity is that difference becomes an end in itself and the unevenness of differential relations evaporates. This paradox is epitomized by Schürmann's perceptive remark that:

> There is no safer formula for social isomorphism than to appeal to everyone's particularity. In claiming one's unique personality, feelings, tastes, lifestyle and beliefs, one does exactly what everyone else does and so promotes uniformity in the very act of denying it. (1986: 305–6)

The least familiar meaning of the subject is the philosophical one. This refers to the thinking subject and the reflection on the nature and conditions of its existence as the location of consciousness. Primarily it is an epistemological category. It is distinguished from the object existing in a reality external to the subject that thinks about it, or indeed from the subject thinking about itself. It is this last meaning that has tended to dominate in the sorts of discussion we have in mind through the identification of a political dimension within it. This takes two forms. One of these is concerned with demonstrating and reporting the failure or exhaustion of the philosophical subject as centre and origin of consciousness, and the authority of the form of truth that can be derived from this. The other takes the form of an attack on the very ambition to constitute or identify a subject as a centre or locus of truth. Taken together, as they often are, this political sense of the subject derived from the philosophical notion of the subject is often referred to as 'de-centring' or 'the de-centred' subject. On this basis the political dimension oscillates between the claim that the philosophical subject cannot be established, and the claim that the philosophical subject should not be established. That is to say, the autonomous self-grounding of consciousness cannot overcome heteronomy, and should not overcome heterogeneity. In this way the fact of the former demonstrates the value of the latter.

On the face of it, this political sense appears to be far from self-evident. It depends on whether one regards a dispute amongst philosophers as political, or whether one assumes that philosophy and politics coincide. However, the case made for the extension of this dispute is by way of reference, with varying degrees of explicitness, to the temporal and spatial location of the philosophical subject. That is to say, to modernity as it emerged in Europe between the sixteenth and seventeenth centuries, and in particular Descartes's solution to the epistemological problem of scepticism and subsequent attempts to ground this solution from Kant to Husserl. In this case the philosophical and grammatical senses coincide in so far as the former is located discursively and modernity is attributed with agency. The force of this reference is such that the claims to a universal status of the modern philosophical subject are disarmed, although this is often conflated with the destruction of universality itself, at the same time as the philosophical subject is subsumed within the familiar list of ills that modernity has bequeathed to the world – capitalism, the atomization of social life, the denigration and destruction of non-modern cultures, the disenchantment of spirituality, the catastrophic desire to master nature, and above all the securing of domination by man – as both determinate cause and adverse effect.

In our view this emphasis upon the political dimension of the philosophical subject is exaggerated and unwarranted. It verifies the philosophical claim to establish the thinking subject as centre or origin simply for the purpose of attacking it. This stems from a petulant rejection of modern rationalism, as if there was something subversive in this gesture, and the desire to identify a foundation for this project which, if removed, would bring about the collapse of the edifice of modernity. This should not, however, be taken as indicative of our support for the defenders of the philosophical subject, such as Habermas. If we are sceptical about the philosophical subject's responsibility for bads, we are equally sceptical about its responsibility for goods. In support of this we can recall a remark by Kristeva, whose work made an important contribution to the launch of the political career of the philosophical subject. For example:

> The present mutations of capitalism, the political and economic reawakening of ancient civilizations (India, China), have thrown into crisis the symbolic systems enclosed in which the Western subject, officially defined as a transcendental subject, has for two thousand years lived out its lifespan. (1975 [1973]: 50)

Within an argument that engages in the political critique of the transcendental subject Kristeva observes that the logic of capital has already rendered this figure obsolete. If we assume with Kristeva, for the sake of argument, that it was once dominant, this is no longer the case. Kristeva's critique, which may well have been otiose in the moment of its enunciation, aimed to champion the existence of the 'speaking subject' against the systematic properties of the symbolic, the 'dominant social code' and the 'Western épistémé' in general. Yet the agency of the 'speaking subject' is located in the logic of capital itself in so far as it annihilates the unitary subject that centres the symbolic. In other words, capital is against the unitary philosophical subject and the symbolic system and for the dislocatory 'subject in process' and the 'affirmative negativity' that this embodies (1998 [1968]). It is for Bataille-style ceaseless expenditure and transgression and against 'the homosexual tendency to identification' – 'the truth of the heterosexual "relation"' – that supports normativity and social normality, and primarily the institution of the family' (157).[2] In this case the political dimension of the critique of the modern philosophical subject as a means of subverting the modernist project, as something that is impossible and as something that is immoral, misfires. Capitalism is already doing the work for us, or at least it was in the euphoric atmosphere of late 1960s permissiveness with its experimental attitude to sexuality, chemicals and performance art that Kristeva championed as a means of liberating signifying practices from their systematic aspect.[3] As a Marxist, and like many of her generation, Kristeva simply took the side of the objective laws of historical development.

Therefore we would claim that it is a waste of time to derive the political subject from the philosophical subject. In this we are assisted by Balibar's recent work (1991, 1994). This demonstrates that, contrary to the tenets of a tradition of philosophical anthropology that culminates in Heidegger, it is simply a mistake to maintain that the notion of the subject as 'thinking thing' originates in Descartes. This confusion arose from an 'objective play on words' attributed to Kant, and which may perhaps be most quickly understood as the effect of problems experienced by Kant in translating Descartes's Latin. The word 'subject' is a translation of both the 'neutral, impersonal notion of a *subjectum*', a metaphysical substance, and the 'personal notion of a *subjectus*: a political and juridical term, which refers to *subjection* or *submission*' (1994: 8). It is the subject in the sense of *subjectus* that Descartes used. Leaving aside Kant's motives for substituting the former for the latter, which Balibar suggests are to do with a desire to substantialize bourgeois citizenship as representative of humanity, and which probably explains the effort made in the political refutation of the philosophical subject, we can consider the structure of Descartes's original formulation. This reveals that a political meaning of the subject grounds Descartes's epistemological and ontological project, and is therefore primary. The reason for this is that Descartes's response to the aporia of doubt took the form of a decision to subordinate, and thus subject, understanding and science to the human individual; but this individual was in turn understood as the *subjectus* of a (divine) sovereign. For Descartes this provided a dimension of certainty and necessity. Consequently, the security of the individual, its escape from scepticism, is grounded in the structure of the substitution 'of an internal center of thought whose structure is that of a sovereign decision, an absent presence, or a source of intelligibility that as such is incomprehensible', or what is commonly referred to as God (1991: 35). Thus in this ontotheological structure *subjectus* is both causality, or origin, and sovereignty, or order.

To get a better sense of what this political meaning is it is worth pursuing Balibar's analysis. Through this structure of substitution the individual acquires the characteristics that had previously been enjoyed by God alone in so far as the individual is subject as *subjectus*. Yet this puts the status of the individual as *subjectus* in question in so far as God is essentially free, the paradigm of free will. Descartes's solution to this problem, which arose from the constraints that surrounded discussion of religion rather than the entailments of logic, was to identify freedom with subjection such that the exercise of free will coincides with 'the act by which God conserves me in a relative perfection' (35) – the existence of perfection being sufficient proof for the existence of God (which Balibar forgets to mention). At the same time the ontotheological structure of substitution is preserved such that 'my subjection to God is the origin of my mastery over and possession of nature' (36). From this Balibar concludes that for modernity 'freedom can only be thought of as the freedom of the *subject*, of the subjected being, that is, as a contradiction in terms' (36) as both active and passive, free and subjected. For example, the subject of the law is also the maker of the law, or, as Balibar notes with respect to Hobbes, the author of the state is also the political actor under the authority of the state (48). Consequently, the name that designates '*originary freedom*' is also the name that politically and historically designated the 'intrinsic limitation of freedom' (1994: 8). However, Balibar's point is that this is only a logical contradiction that stems from the task of overcoming the constraints of thought itself in order to think freedom. This does not mean that this task is without historical effectivity. This is why there is little reason to hope that fomalizable conceptual analysis will resolve matters, as this approach is blind to the historicity of freedom. Rather, the issue is to do with the dynamic of the political subject conceived historically as 'becoming free', and with the maintenance of an inner or outer relation with subjection that this presupposes (9), and through which the subject 'necessarily *subjects himself to himself* or, if you like, performs his own subjection' (10, original emphasis).

With the establishment of this problematic we can consider the third, political meaning of the subject, or the political subject as such. This is familiar through the curious phrase 'loyal subjects'. It denotes a relation of subjection between a subject and some other agency, or even a subject in the grammatical sense in so far as this occurs in political discourse. In Balibar's opinion it is Foucault who has inter-rogated the legacy of this problematic, in that Foucault's work 'is a materialist phenomenology of the transmutation of subjection' (55). This can be confirmed by a clarification in one of Foucault's last essays that it was the subject, and not power, that had served as the central theme of his research. The subject is central for Foucault because it is understood in such a way that it gives rise to a specific form of power that both subjugates and makes subject to. Foucault understands the modern political subject as 'subject to someone else by control and dependence, and tied to his own identity by a conscience or self-knowledge' (Foucault 1982: 212). Yet Foucault departs from the ontotheological inheritance in which this has been understood through the use of a non-substantive notion of power as 'a mode of action which acts on the actions of others' (220). Power is not external to the field of its operation as original cause or ground. The condition of this mode is twofold: firstly, 'the "other" must be thoroughly recognized and maintained to the end as a person who acts'; secondly, faced with a relationship of power, 'a whole field of responses, reactions, results and possible inventions may open up' (220). In short, power is not opposed to freedom, it presupposes it. It is exercised through a network of relations that Foucault calls governance or governmentality that are coextensive with modernity. It takes the form of a relation between the non-determination of the subject and the effort to structure a field of possibilities in order to facilitate social reproduction and cohesion. Political society must include the freedom of the subject, otherwise it would not be reproduced. The slightest change would annihilate it. For Foucault this freedom takes the form of resistance to subjection in so far as this is understood as a positioning and a placing that 'ties the individual to himself and submits him to others in this way' (212) such that we 'refuse what we are' (216), and in particular anything that could be stabilized as an identity. Importantly, recalcitrance is internal to the modern political subject. For this reason it is stupid to regard the representation of the subject in the various versions of the social contract as the ground of the modern political subject. Rather, the social contract is a response to the modern political subject.[4]

With this in mind we can reinscribe the political within the threefold meaning of the subject. The political subject is constituted by and through antagonism. This is because it is not grounded in necessity. Its appearance is a matter of contingency, which is what makes it modern. By this we mean a situation in which an attempt is made to determine its order and the conduct appropriate to it without recourse to pregiven measures or criteria. These may be those that are derived from the order of what has gone before, or tradition, or from an eternal order such as metaphysics – in short, from a discourse that authorizes and determines a place of intelligibility. Such a situation can only arise through the destruction or annihilation of the authority of such criteria, the absence of a ground. This situation is contingent in the sense that it cannot be predicted, but also in the more critical sense that it reveals the contingent or non-necessary character of a ground.[5] That is to say, objectivity is brought into question. This is why Blumenberg, in his reconstruction of the role of nominalist theology in the emergence of modernity, which took the recognition of the contingency of God's decision to create the world as the positive content of its doctrine, could remark that 'nominalism was a system meant to make man extremely uneasy about the world' (1983: 151). Subjection is not given or guaranteed by the political subject but is instead posed by it, as a question. By the same token we can say the same of freedom.

In order to provide a surface for this reinscription we will consider the example of an intervention that attempts to articulate the three meanings of the subject as a means of constructing a relation of equivalence between them – in other words, of eliminating the conflict between these three meanings. This occurs in the work of Laclau and Mouffe (1985) and Laclau (1990). In fact, articulation works as a theoretical object in this intervention, and at two levels. It is used to describe the practice of politics in the absence of a determining ground, or what they understand as 'hegemony'. It is also characteristic of the method that their argument employs, as it too does not derive from a determining ground, and in this sense aspires to be hegemonic. In solidarity with the practice of articulation this inscription takes the form of a *rearticulation* of the tensions in their argument that arise from the presence of the three meanings of the subject within it. The point of departure for this argument is Laclau and Mouffe's account of the relation between the subject and contingency. This is posed in purely political terms in order to secure the dimension of *antagonism*. The presence of this dimension exceeds the limits of the articulation of the subject. It corresponds to the moment of *disarticulation* or *dislocation* that for Laclau and Mouffe characterizes any 'hegemonic crisis'. As we shall see, this hangs on the value of contingency itself, or the historicity through which contingency is made present as the absence of a determining ground – in other words, the modernity of the political subject.

3.2 The Basic Antagonism

Laclau and Mouffe's elaboration of the concept of antagonism is the most productive and intellectually significant aspect of their theoretical intervention as it undermines two assumptions that had hitherto distorted the political nature of the subject. The first of these was that the political subject was necessarily subordinate to either logical or dialectical contradiction, or to 'real opposition', or to 'essential interests' derived from a predetermined ground. The second was that the political nature of the subject is necessarily embodied in some determined figure of judgement, history or action. Both rejections can be summarized in the notion of 'anti-essentialism'. In this respect Laclau and Mouffe go beyond thinking antagonism in terms of a description of the conditions which accompany antagonism to antagonism as such, the point at which familiar narratives of antagonism break off or some *deus ex machina* enters the scene (1985: 124). This is accompanied by an account of the political subject in terms of its relation to antagonism, contingency and modernity. In this section we shall consider the limits of this articulation in their work.

Modernity is present in Laclau and Mouffe's argument as the designation of the scope of its application and the condition of its intelligibility. They point out that 'the hegemonic form of politics only becomes dominant at the beginning of modern times, when the reproduction of the different social areas takes place in permanently changing conditions which constantly require the construction of new systems of differences' (138). Following Lefort, Laclau and Mouffe accept that modernity is characterized by the absence of a 'transcendental guarantor' that would establish a totally unified society (186). Put differently, it is the evacuation of any measure or ground of the social, whether this ground is located transcendentally or in terms of a frontier that marks *this* society from *that* society, or, more commonly, through an inventive combination of both. The recognition of the mundane character of the social is the core achievement of modernity, from which it derives its principle of equality. This is the universal dimension of modernity, even if it is not always accepted by those societies that could otherwise be described as modern, or indeed those who would not describe themselves in this manner. Modern society is constituted around the experience of its own contingency. This means that society is not fully present to itself.

This is explained by reference to premodern societies in which full presence is given by 'the existence of a closed space where each differential position is fixed as a specific and irreplaceable moment' (127). Conflict, which is largely military rather than political, takes place through a relation to an exterior. This exterior can be real, or imagined, or even produced through the expulsion of scapegoats such as the diseased and the mentally unstable. Millenarianism is a typical form of this conflict in which the rural peasant is simply opposed, face to face, to the urban artisan. There is no commonality between them. The space that each occupies is closed and the differences that circulate within them are completely absorbed by themselves in relation to a frontier that determines the negative other. Needless to say, this is a reciprocal relation, demonstrated by the manner in which both artisans and peasants justified themselves through reference to religion, or indeed the authority of a king, or the way that Christians and Muslims were happy to describe each other as infidels. Under these conditions of closure a hierarchical system of differences is rendered equivalent, and thus guarantees the sameness of the social space, by reference to a common frontier with an other. Objectivity, or what is the case, coincides with experience, or what appears to be the case. Alterity is what escapes the same, while at the same time being that which conditions it. The simple dependency of the same on its other is in most cases beyond the grasp of the participants, as the historical reconstructions of the Monty Python films demonstrate.

Laclau and Mouffe describe the introduction of antagonism into this space in the following terms. It is the experience of 'the limit of all objectivity', or when the very contingency of objectivity is experienced as fact. This should not be confused with the experience of a limit or frontier as such. Rather, it is in the order of a confrontation with an internal limit. This is because antagonism is not the impossibility of being two things at once, as in a logical or dialectical contradiction, but the impossibility of being one thing because being a thing depends on a reference to a ground that guarantees the objectivity of anything. Consequently, the 'cause' of antagonism is not to be understood as somehow extra-discursive, like the clash of two stones or the logical incompatibility of concepts. This is not to deny that in reality bricks collide or that people's arguments get confused but simply to point out that these events are not necessarily antagonistic. In this respect antagonism is a specific experience of discursivity in which its contingency becomes manifest – in other words, modernity. It is at this point that the tensions in Laclau and Mouffe's argument that would tend to disarticulate it begin to emerge. Following Butler (1993: 9), we would say that these are organized around the relation between a logic of social practices – or in our terms, the experience of historicity – and a logic to which such practices or experiences are subject, but which is itself not subject to such practices or experiences. As Butler puts it, this suggests that we are asked to accept that logic is not itself 'the distilled and sedimented effect of social practices' (10).

We can follow the lines of this tension through a more fully elaborated theorization of antagonism that Laclau provided in a later text. This enables a firmer hold on the problem of the visibility of its presence in that the definition of antagonism as 'the limit of all objectivity' means exactly what it says: 'Antagonism does not have an objective meaning, but is that which prevents the constitution of objectivity itself' (Laclau 1990: 17). In this respect the defining characteristic of antagonism is that it reveals the 'ultimately contingent nature of all objectivity' (18). Hence the dimension of contingency is decisive in so far as antagonism reveals the impossibility of *either* full presence *or* absence or lack. It is simply the impossibility of objectivity itself: which is to say, no pure anything at all but no pure nothing either, the constitutive errancy of the structure presumed by the thesis of the simultaneous impossibility/possibility of society. By conceptualizing antagonism in terms of the simultaneity of affirmation and negation Laclau and Mouffe radicalize the rationalistic notion of contingency, the mode of existence of an entity that cannot be reduced to the metaphysical ground of an essence. The contingent is not that which is random, as in a statistical sample of foreign-born taxpayers or registered voters, but rather, that which simultaneously could or could not exist. It is thus purely exceptional as no necessity guarantees its appearance, possible rather than probable. Antagonism is not an actuarial matter. This is both cause and consequence of Laclau and Mouffe's anti-essentialism. There is no privileged differential position or subject of antagonism that would stand in for or regulate it as it affects all differences within a historically specific conjuncture. This does not mean that contingency is experienced equally across the social terrain. Rather, the objectivity of the differential relations in which subjects are located collapses. It is a crisis at the level of existing social totality that can only announce its disruptive presence indirectly: for example, in the form of metaphor.[6] It is not reducible to the nature of the antagonistic elements as if it was a question of disposition, like the description of militant workers as antagonistic that one finds in the files of personnel managers. Antagonism is nothing personal.

We have no disagreement with this definition and its consequences. Our question is as follows. Is this a logical definition of antagonism beyond the horizon of all possible experience; or is it a specific effect of the historicity of the attempt to construct objectivity on the basis of its very contingency, and thus of the exposure of the contingency of objectivity itself, the constitutive contamination of objectivity by the impurity of power in the sense of 'power to' as distinct from power understood as 'power over'? We believe that it is the latter case, and in this respect Laclau and Mouffe's position is closer to Foucault's account of the modern political subject than one would otherwise have thought. Indeed, if 'power over' was totally determining, then it could not be exercised. Recalcitrance would be impossible. Objectivity and experience would be undifferentiated and any differential hierarchy would be understood in terms of the 'order of things'. Conflict would take on its old premodern millenarian form, or would be understood through the contemporary manifestations of this paradigm such as religious and ethnic fundamentalism.

Although presupposed by the concept and scope of application of antagonism, the nature of the political subject is more or less systematically occulted in Laclau and Mouffe's account. In any event, whatever presence it enjoys, it is not theoretically secured. This is because Laclau and Mouffe also wish to assert the priority of the discursive, and thus the grammatical subject that goes with it. This has the effect of flattening the notion of the discursive such that discourses are abstracted from the specificity of the conjuncture in which they are constituted, as if all discourse follows the same logic or 'grammar', and thus the political dimension of discourse is removed. It is an approach that depends on a pragmatic account of discourse, as found, for example, in Wittgenstein's notion of 'language games' (1983), wherein the nature of discourse is plural in the sense that there is always more than one discourse and the nature of any one discourse cannot be reduced to a single ground or determination – for example, in terms of utilitarian, rationalistic or teleological purpose. There is always more than one thing to do, and always more than one way of doing it. The nature of a particular discourse can only be determined descriptively, with all the problems this entails of an infinite regression concerning the discourse through which description takes place. The description is as contingent as the discourse it describes. Consequently, discourse is a question of convention or propriety.

On this basis subjectivity is understood within the intuitive terms of a certain practical disposition. This is expressed through the employment of the notion of subject-position which becomes deprived of the radically historicist dimension that Laclau and Mouffe believe that it enjoys. Subject-positions are understood to be constituted within discursive processes and any appeal to a non-discursive vantage point in order to ground such positions is illegitimate (1985: 115). The inherent weakness in this approach is the reduction of subject-positions to discourses understood as self-contained structures, wherein by simply being a determinate effect of a discursive structure the distinction between subject-position and structure collapses and the dimension of constitution becomes otiose. It resembles the conservative belief, embodied in the sociologism of ethnomethodology or systems theory, that the world is a seamless whole effortlessly self-organized by the people that inhabit it. Ceaselessly reproducing itself in the face of the problems that it encounters, this picture of discourse is dependent upon the success of what Althusser referred to as the 'ideology of practice'.[7] There is no place in it for conflict or antagonism of any sort as tasks are simply accomplished to make way for more tasks to be done. In this world politics does not occur, except perhaps as a consequence of mismanagement.

Undoubtedly, reliance on the pragmatist account provides the advantage of not having to refer to an extra-discursive ground of discourse. Discourse is contingent, but in itself this does not provide a specifically *political* sense of contingency. It is simply a logical statement. It is one thing to understand contingency as the acceptance of the *facticity* of material existence and thus the purely conventional and pragmatic forms through which this existence is organized. This is one possible consequence to be drawn from Heidegger's doctrine of *Dasein's* 'thrownness'. However, this element of contingency does not necessarily determine the subject as a political subject. Sociologism can easily provide numerous examples of discourses and the subjects that bear them that function in an eminently practical manner, even if the 'negotiations' of those subjects are subsumed under the ethos of pragmatism. Yet it is a very different matter if one refers to the contingent nature of the authority which legitimates these forms of existence against other equally contingent alternatives, or the contingency of those discourses through which order is established.

These two senses of contingency are conflated in Laclau and Mouffe. Indeed, the two senses of contingency are in conflict and as such constitute the internal limit or antagonism of Laclau and Mouffe's theory, the point at which it becomes disarticulated from itself and the objectivity of its hegemonic frontier collapses. Pragmatism provides the element of objectivity that antagonism denies and as such denies the presence of power in the constitution of discourse itself. On the pragmatist account politics only exists in the banal sense of the maintenance of particular hegemonic articulations, or the objectification of difference as equivalence. Antagonism is not present within this scenario. Pragmatism and antagonism are articulated through the sense of contingency that each involves, but if the political sense of contingency is to be preserved then these senses have to be differentiated. It is the second sense of contingency that is the political one. It is political because it shows, in addition to the facticity of discourse, the non-necessary character of the discourse in which any particular subject is situated in so far as this situation is characterized by a differential hierarchy or, to put the same thing differently, the presence of power. Therefore, a specific experience of contingency is required in order to identify the political nature of the subject. Laclau and Mouffe have provided it in the concept of antagonism, yet this does not require a pragmatist foundation in the capacity of subjects to get on with the tasks in hand. If anything, it undermines it.

In a later text Laclau attempted to reconcile these two senses of contingency by insisting that 'there is no source of the social different from people's decisions in the process of the social construction of their own identity and their own existence' (1990: 192). This statement attempts to overcome the problem of the two sense of contingency by identifying the logical with the social. No political consequences actually follow from the doctrine of social constructionism. It is fully reconcilable with the pragmatic fact that subjects straightforwardly proceed with the task of constructing society and their own hierarchically organized positions within it, whether they are aware of any of this or not. It does not follow from the premise of social constructionism that all members of a society that exists through the discourses that constitute it will have equal opportunity or capacity to construct their own identity or existence. Therefore, the introduction of the political sense of contingency requires that the objective status accorded to the plurality of decisions that are supposed to constitute society has to be negated in some way. To do this we can reiterate that the notion of contingency connected to the experience of the political subject that arises through modernity is not equivalent to the notion of contingency that arises through reference to a multiplicity of subject-positions participating in a plurality of language games. The subject has become a position. Yet it is not entirely unconnected either. The difference is located in the fact that the latter refers to the sedimentation of contingency, its taken-for-granted status. In other words, to the transformation of *historicity* into history, or the collapse of logical explanation into historical narratives.

Laclau and Mouffe provide an example that is given the task of securing this collapse. This is the foundation of the Welfare State within the nineteenth-century structuring of European political space through the revolutionary opposition between '*anciens régimes*' and 'the people', and in particular Disraeli's inscription of this division within social space under the slogan 'One Nation'. This allowed for the 'differential absorption of demands' (1985: 130) and prevented the reactivation of a millenarian-style conflict *within the social space.* Differences remained differential but were denied any relation to a negativity opposed to this space that could be located within it. They were flattened through equivalence. Instead, antagonism became displaced to the 'frontier of the social' as a means of *guaranteeing the objectivity of that social space.* In other words, a premodern millenarian-style conflict is reinvented within modernity itself in order to objectify hierarchical and unequal relations of difference. To be sure, these differences were not that complex, being largely a question of 'class struggle'. Yet the point is that this was a political solution designed to prevent the emergence of antagonism or the political as such. It was simply pragmatic to do so, although historians of the period would quite easily point out the various ways in which antagonism persisted within the social space despite 'One Nation' rhetoric. Moreover, this frontier of the social enjoyed the empirical and 'objective' status of 'The Empire'.

Laclau and Mouffe's account of the significance of this episode is curious. Intellectually, this development corresponds to the 'moment of the positivist illusion that the ensemble of the social can be absorbed in the intelligible and ordered framework of a society' (130). Here, the positivist reinvention of the fullness of society is considered to be an illusion that enjoys the status of objective and 'natural' fact. Aside from the problem of whether intellectual and political developments can be coordinated in this way, which would raise interminable reflexive problems for the status of Laclau and Mouffe's own theory, this illusion is articulated within Laclau and Mouffe's argument as, almost immediately, it is elevated to the level of political and theoretical necessity. Thus they assert that the 'relative closure' of the social space 'is necessary for the discursive construction of the antagonism, given that the delimitation of a certain interiority is required to construct a totality permitting the division of the space into two camps' (132). Thus, in addition to the sedimentation of contingency at the historical level this statement serves to demonstrate *the sedimentation of antagonism at the political-theoretical level.* Antagonism as that which brings objectivity into question is substituted for antagonism *as the ground of objectivity.* In so far as history is the privileged terrain of determination, this corresponds to the absorption of class struggle within the procedures of the Welfare State, or the era of 'consensus'. In fact, antagonism guarantees the objectivity of the social on two fronts: within the social, and between the social and something deemed to be external to it. At this point the notion of antagonism loses its critical-political value. Antagonism is articulated within a hegemonic regime as that which stabilizes it, or as its centre. In this sense we can refer to *hegemonic antagonisms*.

There are two critical consequences that issue from this. Despite Laclau and Mouffe's advances in the theorization of antagonism it remains thought within the political understood as an exterior/interior relation, a nostalgia for the social body. Secondly, the account of the subject is split, not by reference to a logic of the subject, but by reference to an account of the social that derives from its historical form as a necessarily closed space, and which Laclau and Mouffe maintain is in fact illusory. Laclau and Mouffe support the necessity of the illusion of social closure, or belief in its objective status, through the argument that without a centre chains of equivalence, through which differences are stabilized, will be difficult to construct. The production of difference will exceed any principle of termination and hegemony will not occur. As Marx put it, 'All that is solid melts into air, all that is holy is profaned.' In fact, Laclau and Mouffe are so concerned by the possibility that this will happen that the absence of social closure is equated with the Gramscian notion of 'organic crisis'. Yet in the moment that this is articulated a further distinction is introduced that complicates matters even further. This rests on the determination of the subject under such conditions through the distinction between the *popular* and the *democratic* subject, and which we would translate as the distinction between the pragmatic and the political subject. To put the matter graphically, the democratic subject thrives through the production of difference that exceeds any termination through reference to a centre, or to a principle through which objectivity is instituted. It is formed through the constant displacement of objectivity, including the objectivity of difference itself, such that difference ceases 'to be grounded upon an *evident and given* separation, in a referential framework acquired once and for all' (134, original emphasis). In short, the democratic subject is equated with antagonism. We might say that the radicality of the democratic subject is located in its performativity, or, to be more precise, the failure or 'infelicity' of its performativity, to use Austin's expression. This is the failure of enunciation, the failure to occupy a place from which one may speak and be recognized, of not being placed where one should be in order to be interpellated as what one ought to be.[8] In other words, subject-positions are denied any objective status and no subject-position can be regarded as separate or autonomous. It is political by virtue of its very anonymity, which is to say that it is not a position at all.

Against this, Laclau and Mouffe assert the priority of the *popular* subject-position. In one sense this corresponds to the continuation of the Marxist doctrine of the increasing polarization of class conflict by non-economic means, as their indebtedness to the 'mythical' Marxism of Luxembourg and Sorel demonstrates. Yet there is nothing particularly democratic about it as its purpose is to ensure the closure of social space. As distinct from antagonism, the *popular* subject-position is performed through the enactment of a decision. This occurs in those situations where 'a political logic *tends* to bridge the gap between political space and society as an empirical referent' (133, original emphasis). As is well known, in this situation differences that cannot be reconciled with empirical social space empirically disappear. We would say that this means that the persistence of differences that cannot be terminated is in itself antagonistic. By the same token, differences that do appear are 'objective'. By means of their differential equivalence they enjoy the dimension of plenitude that their being articulated provides for the social space. Performatively, they are felicitous. They correspond to the pragmatist notion of the subject-position in which there is no distinction between the saying and the said. To explore the consequences of this opposition we shall expand the field of its inscription by examining the effects that Laclau and Mouffe's intervention has produced in the theory of the subject. This turns on the very objectivity of the subject itself – that is to say, on the presumption of its fullness.

3.3 Outing the Subject

Laclau and Mouffe's account of antagonism and subjectivity has been attacked from a variety of perspectives. We suspect that this is because there is something very antagonistic about it. This is its chief virtue. On the other hand, its aspiration to be hegemonic is its major vice, although luckily it has not succeeded in reducing theoretical discussion to a relation of equivalence. Differential antagonisms persist. In considering these we wish to defend the relation between modernity, antagonism and the democratic political subject that Laclau and Mouffe have established. As should be clear, this is at the cost of their investment in the relation between 'hegemony and socialist strategy' but not, we would argue, in the notion of a 'radical democratic socialist politics'. This issue turns on the extent to which such a politics can be enunciated from a position of fullness. In so far as it cannot, then the democratic dimension of the political has a good chance. The attacks on Laclau and Mouffe that we consider reverse this democratic perspective. That is to say, they revert from the perspective of the emergence of an errant subject through the limit of the social, or the limit of objectivity, to the security of the fullness of the social from the objectivity of the subject that enunciates it. This objectivity is condensed in the notion of identity. In various ways identity is given as a desirable ethical and political good on the basis that it exists, and that it exists in a plural manner such that each identity is unique or different. An affirmative 'politics of identity' or 'politics of difference' arises from this, in which negativity is regarded as an exterior phenomenon. Hence antagonism is simply a relation between identities or alliances of identities. We would argue the opposite. There can only be a 'politics of identity' in so far as the political dimension is located within identity itself, which is to say the existence of an identity is in question.

For example, Landry and Maclean dismiss the notion of antagonism on the basis that it is abstract. This abstract nature is alleged to arise from Laclau and Mouffe's reliance on a totalizing model that is 'as homologous as the traditional sociological models of "society" that they set out to displace' (1991: 43). The effect of this is to deny, marginalize, silence, etc. 'some of those very subject positions that their theory of hegemony is seeking to articulate' (47). In other words, Laclau and Mouffe are not popular enough as they undermine 'the autonomous self-understanding of social movements' (49–50). This tactical inflation of the effectivity of theoretical discourse is the catalyst for the hallucination that Laclau and Mouffe are complicit with 'the emergence of "democracy" as a new global myth and rhetorical alibi for multinational capitalism' (59). Through this juvenile and shameful allegation Landry and Maclean assert the priority of the popular over the democratic subject. In effect, Landry and Maclean transfer the fullness of the totalizing model to popular subjects themselves. Somewhat perversely, this is grounded through reference to the Lacanian notion of the Subject, which they oppose to a historicist notion of subject-position. Presumably, this means that autonomous self-understanding is naturally Lacanian. The argument is that subject-positions, in so far as these derive from historically specific relations of power, are various corruptions of an original and authentic Subject. Hence, it only remains for subject-positions to be eliminated and the Subject will be released back into a state of authentic and original innocence from where it had been taken. After all, what could be more popular? As we shall see below, the last thing anyone would want to see is the presentation of the Lacanian Subject in all its phenomenological glory, in so far as anyone agrees on what this notion means.

Yet Laclau and Mouffe should take some responsibility for this voluntaristic populism as in fact both senses of the subject, the Lacanian Subject and the historicist subject-position, are present in their argument. Smith (1998) has attempted to mediate this inconsistency by adopting a 'radical democratic pluralist' position that is opposed to Laclau and Mouffe's 'radical democratic socialism'. The vehicle for this is a distinction between 'structural' and 'subject' position. A structural position refers to the objective dimension of an individual's existence but very little is said about this. A subject-position refers to 'the ensemble of beliefs through which an individual interprets and responds to her structural positions within a social formation' (58). These beliefs are not rigidly deterministic but allow of what Bourdieu referred to as 'regulated improvisations' (64). It is the validity of subject-positions that Smith wishes to defend in the name of pluralism. The advantage of subject-positions is that they may be shared by individuals – Smith stipulates at least two – in a manner that does not correspond to the structural position that individuals also occupy. The question of the relation between structural positions and pluralism is ring-fenced in Smith's argument.[9]

On this account antagonism is located at the level of belief. It arises as a threat to a subject position in the form of 'a relation that is denying her identity, as something that is blocking herself from realizing what she regards as her true potential and stopping her society from becoming an ideal social order' (67). In other words, antagonism is a threat to self-understanding or social status. It prevents one from being who one would like to be and would like to be recognized by others as being, or from getting one's own way. Yet an ambiguity remains concerning the precise source of the dimension of negativity. A subject may perceive herself as threatened by something external to her but it does not follow that either the threat or the source of the threat actually exists because it cannot be shown to be independent of her beliefs. In fact, it may even constitute her beliefs. In which case, the experience of antagonism would be purely self-serving. Smith is somewhat coy on this issue. Individuals are understood as being caught up in an interminable search for identity. This search is the individual's life-work, as no set of beliefs will ever fully explain her structural positioning.[10] There are no antagonistic consequences to be drawn from this. Rather, 'every subject remains somewhat alienated and restless, for she can never be "at home" in her largely determined structural positionings' (68). Thus, individuals are only antagonistic if their coping mechanisms are threatened, and not by virtue of the alienated structure of their subjectivity. Yet the only account of the subject that Smith provides is in terms of its essentially alienated nature.

Here the Marxist notion of alienation is reduced to its purely 'humanistic' content and elevated to a universal status that corresponds to the commonality of adolescent experience in postwar liberal democracies. This is mirrored by the claim that each subject-position has its own version of what is universal that it attempts to realize. Even this is not the source of antagonism, which is surprising as this universality would have to be realized over and against the other universalities presupposed by the plurality of subject-positions. Thus identities are innocent of hegemonic ambition. They are havens of purity that empower individuals to cope with their alienated existence. This draining of Marxism to its humanistic corpse is reinforced by Smith's disavowal of her reliance on Marxist anti-humanism. Although Smith takes great pains to reject any debt to Marxism, the account of what a subject-position does is a reformulation of Althusser's definition of ideology as an imaginary relation to real conditions, i.e. structural position. This is reinforced by the claim that individuals identify with their subject-position rather than their structural position through the Althusserian mechanism of interpellation. However, instead of understanding identification as mis-identification, as in the Althusserian model, identification is regarded as a good and healthy thing. The disavowal of the critical consequences of the Althusserian account of ideology is explicit in Smith's frustration with the presence of the Lacanian framework from which it is derived in Laclau and Mouffe. This is because the Lacanian framework understands identification to be predicated on a structure of fantasy that compensates for individual inadequacy. Consequently, the pragmatic beliefs through which an individual 'realizes her true potential' are fantasies, which is to say that the idea that the individual is possessed of a hidden potential that could be expressed positively is equally fantastic.[11] Instead of confronting this problem, Smith adopts a more diplomatic solution and relativizes the problem to a question of emphasis. Hence Smith's emphasis on the critique of economism in Laclau and Mouffe which is celebrated in her account of their work.

To be sure, this had the effect of eliminating the lingering notion of an essential class-belonging from which political agency could be derived. Yet this is undermined through the replacement of class essentialism with an anaemic essentialism of the liberal individual's compulsion to be optimistic.

At this point we could deepen our critique of Smith's pluralism by revealing its complicity with managerialism or multiculturalism. Our argument would be that it 'acts out' the substitution of politics with the disciplinary mechanisms of therapy and speech codes. Being or having an identity is a purely pragmatic matter. It is better to have one than not have one as this is what multicultural society esteems above all. However, to move the discussion along we will instead return to the pertinence of the distinction between Subject and subject-position that was so rigorously misunderstood in Landry and Maclean, who simply used it to sustain the fantasy of an un-alienated individual. Doing this will provide us with another perspective on the relation between antagonism and the subject. Specifically, this is with reference to Žižek's critique of Laclau and Mouffe, in which the problem of the presence of both a Lacanian notion of the Subject and a historicist notion of subject-position in their argument is squarely confronted. In other words, Žižek confronts the antagonism in the theory of antagonism.

To frame Žižek's critique we can say that, as a rough guide, the notion of the Subject is the device through which individuals are inscribed within a universe of meaning or symbolic structure. This is the location of subject-positions that are occupied so that individuals may enjoy both a minimum of meaningful social existence and their subjection to the operations of power through which stable social existence is reproduced. Thus it is subject-positions that are the objects of hegemonic strategy. Consequently, hegemony is ideological in the Althusserian sense of eternal, a point borne out by Laclau's subsequent remarks concerning the necessity of ideology. This does not mean, however, that there is anything counter-hegemonic about the Subject. The Subject is both the condition of possibility and impossibility of hegemony in so far as hegemony requires interpellation and the failure of interpellation. This failure corresponds to the emergence of the void that the Subject is within any symbolic structure as, by definition, the Subject cannot be symbolized or reconciled with a universe of meaning. In Lacanian terms, Žižek refers to this as the Real. Importantly, Žižek overcomes the problem that undermined Althusser's notion of interpellation by applying the Lacanian notion of the Subject in a more consistent manner. Whereas Althusser was unable to conceive of the Subject before its interpellation in any positive sense, and thus left unanswered the question as to what exactly is the thing that is interpellated, Žižek turns this inability into a positive dimension. It is precisely because there is nothing there that interpellation occurs. The Subject is a void. Interpellation and the subject-positions that arise through it are concerned to cover over this traumatic fact, in the same way that the traumas that mess up the analysand are merely symptoms that repress the traumatic truth that his or her life actually is awful. The Subject is neither the locus of authentic freedom nor true potential.

The consequences that Žižek draws in theorizing antagonism are derived from what psychoanalysis takes as fact: namely, that individuals can never be who they would prefer themselves to be recognized as being, both by themselves and others, and, following the logic of psychoanalysis, are in fact constituted by the repression of this traumatic fact. This applies as much to the heroes of global capital like Bill Gates as to the innocent Third World peasant deprived of his or her land rights. Both are equally deluded in their belief that they have a place in the symbolic order that they, or the 'culture' to which they are subordinate, have determined. Self-understanding is derived from narcissism. The consequences of this are clear. For example: 'The feminist struggle against patriarchal, male chauvinist oppression is necessarily filled out by the *illusion* that afterwards, when patriarchal oppression is abolished, women will finally achieve their full identity with themselves, realize their human potentials, etc.' (Žižek 1990: 251, original emphasis). According to Žižek, this means that antagonism is simply a 'self-inflicted impediment' (252) which occurs precisely when an external enemy is eliminated as one can no longer maintain one's unhappiness by the detour or the alibi of the other. 'The moment of victory is the moment of greatest loss' (252) or, in Hegelian terms, 'the loss of the loss'. Subject-positions – downsized middle-class white male, crack addict, New Age psychotherapist, cyborg, lieutenant in the Nation of Islam or childless woman in her late thirties – are simply devices designed to avoid this experience. On this account identities have no integrity or status.

Through this intervention Žižek distinguishes between two types of antagonism and establishes a hierarchy between them. Any antagonistic relations which subject-positions or social identities happen to enjoy with each other are merely doing the work of ideology in pluralist societies. Žižek refers to this as 'the social *reality* of the antagonistic fight' (253, original emphasis). This point is similar to the one that we have made above concerning *hegemonic antagonisms* and popular subjects. Against this, Žižek poses the experience of 'pure antagonism', which is derived from the Lacanian notion of the Subject as a void. This is because the Subject cannot be subjectivated, cannot have a place. According to Žižek, the Subject is:

> *beyond or before subjectivation* [i.e. subject-position, JV]: subjectivation designates the movement through which the Subject integrates what is given him/her into the universe of meaning – this integration always ultimately fails, there is a certain left-over which cannot be integrated into the symbolic universe, an object which resists subjectivation, and the Subject is precisely correlative to this object. (254, emphasis added)

For Žižek the Subject constitutes the impossibility of subject-position as a fully enclosed self-sufficient entity. Subject-position is merely the aim of an imaginary identification, to use the Lacanian vocabulary, or what the Subject desires to be. This is revealed through the experience of 'pure antagonism'. It is the failure of the Subject to occupy the place designated for it within the symbolic or, to put the same thing differently, the experience of not having a place. Hence the Subject is the experience of 'pure antagonism', an empty place which prevents the closure of the symbolic in which an individual would find himself or herself subjectivated. The 'left-over' that antagonism reveals is an object to which the Subject is 'correlative' – except, one should add, that this Subject is no longer a Subject but an 'object' and the objectivity of this object is measured by its distance from its determination by the symbolic, or what Žižek, following Lacan, calls the Other. This is why on other occasions Žižek refers to this object as a stain; it's there, but you would rather it wasn't. This would suggest that the Subject actually is 'pure antagonism' and, further, that this correspondence takes place in the same moment in which the existence of the Subject is revealed as the failure of the place it would occupy.

On this score two critical points need to be made immediately. Firstly, the existence of antagonism requires the persistence of a measure or ground that is falsified by antagonism, as it reveals that the Subject fails to 'measure up' to it. This ground is the symbolic understood as structure of meaning and meaningful relations in which the Subject fails to take its place or, more accurately, is produced in the moment of this failure. The presence of the Subject takes the form of the remainder of any symbolic order as the internal limit of the social or the 'internal impossibility of the Other' (254). Secondly, contrary to

Žižek's claim, antagonism does not in fact appear 'as such' or in a pure state. Rather, what emerges has the status of the 'object' that simply measures the distance of the Subject from the objectivity provided by the symbolic realm. This has the status of the symptom, which on at least one occasion Žižek has suggested should be enjoyed. As a political style this requires that one counters the objectivity of the symbolic by deepening one's sense of alienation, even in the form of hyperbolic conformity. The political is thus constrained to a mimetic presence. There is no failure of objectivity, and thus of a ground or measure, in Žižek's account. Maintaining this relation between the Subject and its failure as the a priori ground of antagonism simply reinscribes the notion of antagonism within the logic of contradiction as the impossibility of being two things at once – precisely, a Subject and a subject-position – rather than as the impossibility of being one thing because being anything depends on a relation to objectivity that antagonism brings into question. Consequently we must dispense with Žižek's notion of 'pure antagonism'. Antagonism is anything but pure.

3.4 Who Wants to be Popular?

We would concede that Žižek's account of the failure of the Subject and its position is very useful in undermining the self-confidence of popular subjects, or at least in confirming the suspicion that these are maintained through the cultivation of delusion. As readers of Žižek would appreciate, this takes place through the vehicle of humour and produces some extremely provocative insights concerning the relation between popular culture, pathological morality and Western meta-physics. We would not wish to denigrate this aspect of his enterprise, and would more or less agree with his recent critique of the ideological role of 'multiculturalism' in the reproduction of global capitalism (1997). The virtue of Žižek's work is that it contests the distribution of appearances, but this is at the price of re-inscribing the necessity of this distribution – in other words, the necessity of the symbolic which the Subject fails to measure up to. Through the mechanism of *suture* the Subject propels itself into a 'universe of meaning' that ultimately evades its grasp. It is only on this basis that Žižek can refer to the Subject at all. The effect of this maintenance is that the psychoanalytic explanation of the constitution of *its* subject functions as an account of the discursive constitution of society. However, if the foundational nature of society is illusory, then it cannot be explanatory.

Ultimately this rests on a naturalist basis and is consistent with

Laclau and Mouffe's assertion of the universal principle that 'every language and every society are constituted as a repression of the consciousness of the impossibility that penetrates them' (Laclau and Mouffe 1985: 125). Given Laclau and Mouffe's correct rejection of analogies with bricks or concepts in the explanation of antagonism, this principle tarnishes their reputation of having broken with essentialist or reductionist accounts of social and political phenomena. It occults the historically specific dimension of contingency through which it acquires a political value. Put another way, this principle is one that only moderns would assert to describe both modernity and any society that fancies itself as non-modern, or to tell such societies what they would prefer not to know about themselves. This occultation is present to the extent that hegemony acquires a normative value. To indulge a caricature, hegemony is understood as working by mobilizing the failed narcissism of self-fulfillment, the failed objectivity of a subject, in order to secure the discipline of its denial; Subjects must misrecognize themselves as self-constituting in order to be articulated with the promise of the fulfillment of this fantasy. This has the effect of equating the political with ideology, and thus of abolishing the difference.[12]

In this respect Žižek's critique of ideology is at the same time a critique of hegemony in that the two terms are synonymous. The reduction of antagonism to the relations between popular positions designated by the symbolic is a fundamental ideological manœuvre that obscures the presence of the political. Does this mean that Žižek provides a clearer grasp of the political subject on the basis of the Lacanian account of the Subject, or is it similarly occulted through the assumption of the inevitability of its failure? To the best of our knowledge, Žižek does not provide a basis on which to answer this question. Instead, his argument, and the political reputation of psychoanalysis in general, proceeds by exploiting the political connotations of psychoanalytic terms which are subsequently transferred to any subject in the grammatical sense that happens to enjoy a conventional political status. This does little more than contribute to the ridiculing of these subjects, albeit under the auspices of a tolerant liberal democracy. Before tackling the question of the political subject and its relation to democracy we should perhaps say a bit more about the psychoanalytical exploitation of the political connotations of some of its terms or, to say the same thing differently, its place within the symbolic that it does not determine.

The basis of this strategy is evident in Žižek's socialization of the

Lacanian category of 'the Real' by way of Hegel's dialectic, a defining aspect of all of his works. The modality of 'the Real' is usually cast in ominous terms. Society and the individuals that comprise it are dedicated to its elimination, suggesting that its presence could be the locus of dislocatory effects. This is because, as Lacan put it, 'The Real resists symbolization absolutely' (1988: 39). This formula re-produces the same problem we have identified with the notion of the Subject such that it is difficult to distinguish between them, a problem that probably arises from the impetus behind the circulation of Lacan's theoretical economy. The problem is that we can only know this about 'the Real' and its property of resistance with reference to the Symbolic in so far as symbolization fails. In which case, the failure of symbolization can only be shown through the Symbolic. The stain turns out actually to have a place. It is a property of the Symbolic, internal to it in so far as it possesses the properties of an entity. This is a function of the Lacanian attribution of systematicity to the Symbolic itself, which it inherited from structural anthropology. Here we can refer to Cornell's devastating critique of the infinite regress that arises from the valorization of 'the Real' (1995). This shows that the alterity invested in 'the Real' is not radical enough, especially in so far as Lacan attempts to ground a transcendental deduction in a circular argument; for example, the phallus guarantees the unity of the symbolic because this is the way that the phallus is symbolized (1995: 771). After all, why would Lacan wish to ascribe the capacity of resistance to 'the Real' other than to symbolize its exteriority to the symbolic? If it is symbolizable, then it is within the symbolic.

In other words, when Lacan and Lacanians imagine that they have discovered a point of absolute distance from the Symbolic they find themselves locked tightly within it. Part of the popularity of this perspective arises from the political connotations of the notion of 'resistance' and its correlate, 'repression'. To interrogate how this works we can consider Copjec's attack on Foucaultian historicism (1994). This comes from a less humorous but more militant Lacanian perspective than Žižek's, and thus possesses the advantages of trans-parency. Copjec's point of intervention turns on the political signifi-cance of Freud's interpretation of the hysterical woman. Against what Copjec claims Foucault's interpretation would be – that the individual subjectivated by the category of the hysteric actually identifies with this category in its subordination to normative disciplinary power (41)[13] – Copjec asserts the superiority of psychoanalysis on the grounds that 'hysteria is conceived by psychoanalysis as a challenge to the subject's social identity: hysteria is the first analyzed instance of the subject's essential division, its questioning and refusal of social dictates' (51). In this, psychoanalysis takes responsibility for the Subject in a gesture that is meant to demonstrate its existence. It thereby claims to know its 'point of view' and to articulate its meaning. In this the Subject acquires a political value as a locus of resistance that psychoanalysis liberates.

Copjec's claim provokes the question of the specificity of enunciation, and in particular of who is doing the analyzing and what is being resisted? Certainly this is not something that could be said on the basis of Freud's views on the hysteric, which in addition to being historically specific are easily located in terms of their subordination to social dictates. For example:

> The majority of hysterical women are among the attractive and even beautiful representatives of their sex, while, on the other hand, the frequency of ugliness, organic defects and infirmities in the lower classes of society does not increase the incidence of neurotic illness among them. (Freud 1984 [1914]: 14)

We are not throwing Freud's evident sexism against the politically progressive claims made on behalf of psychoanalysis. Others have done this more effectively. Undoubtedly Freud was a *petit-bourgeois* moralist who, despite some inflated references to the heritage of Western civilization – Moses, Sophocles, Shakespeare – never managed to transcend the horizon of interpretation determined by modernist melodrama and its concern with the unstable borders between domestic and social humiliation.[14] Neither do we seek to rely on the fact that Freud's case histories on hysteria demonstrate that it is the unfortunate analysand who is resisting Freud's views on social dictates. Rather, we would question the political purchase of psychoanalysis on the basis of the assumptions that have accumulated around the inevitability of resistance, assuming that this takes place. It is this very inevitability that deprives the political claims of psychoanalysis of any purchase because, at best, it is subordinate to the psychoanalytical account of the Subject in the sense that it is necessary for the coherency of this account. Therefore, to make the Subject a locus of freedom innocent of relations of power that psychoanalysis liberates is to convert the Subject into a popular subject.[15] As Butler has argued, there is no reason why the unconscious is any less structured by power relations than the position of the subject. To reiterate her question: 'If we find an attachment to subjection at the level of the unconscious, what kind of resistance is to be wrought from that?' (1997b: 88). In short, a priori resistance is futile as, although establishing the 'incomplete character of any effort to produce a subject by disciplinary means' – although we would go further and claim that the notion of resistance completes the psychoanalytical subject – it is impotent in the face of the 'dominant terms of productive power' (89). These terms are beyond the grasp of psychoanalysis in so far as society is simply understood as constituted by the repression of something so terrible it cannot even be named. Indeed, this is explicit in Copjec, where it takes the form of a categorical imperative; there must be repression so that psychoanalysis can be true (1994: 24).

Perhaps the most devastating critique of the alleged relation between psychoanalysis and politics in which the above critiques are subsumed remains the charge that this relation relies on a series of analogies between the psychic and the social through which this relation is 'acted out'. The validity of this critique does not depend upon the observation that reasoning through analogy is weak and unpersuasive, such that anything can be made analogous with almost anything else, although this charge is no less true. In the case of psychoanalysis this is effected through a generalization of the grammatical subject and at the same time the subordination of this subject to the philosophical subject and the impossibility of its self-constitution. Rather, the point is that the assumption that society and the individuals that comprise it is composed of a series of instances that can enjoy mutual relations of analogy and which can be subsumed through an analogy with a whole or a totality is unsustainable. This assumption is positively medieval. Its persistence reinscribes a nostalgia for the body. It is not so much that Freud and his subsequent followers have failed to show the relation between the psychic and the social, but more that they have failed to make the distinction or to identify the psychic as such.

In the case of Laclau and Mouffe the attachment to psychoanalysis acts as a drag on their innovative theorization of the political subject (Bellamy 1993: 34) and the concept of antagonism. This becomes critical when they come to consider the political nature of postmodernity as this remains overdetermined by an assumption of the coincidence between logic and historicity, or between sense and being. The collapse of the 'Welfare State' and the 'positivist illusion' that rendered necessary the illusion that the 'Welfare State' had managed to constitute itself around a series of hegemonic antagonisms is simply a moment in the unfolding of a teleology of 'complexity'. 'Complexity' coincides with itself through a destabilization and displacement of frontiers as these cease to be 'grounded upon an *evident and given* separation, in a referential framework acquired once and for all' (Laclau and Mouffe 1985: 134, original emphasis). In other words, the collapse of the objectivity of the social is at the same time an expression of the objectivity of the social itself. The social is the agent of its own complexification. At one level this allows a privilege to be accorded to the democratic subject over the popular subject, yet only in so far as it occupies the site of an antagonism between two logical incompatibles: namely, equivalence and difference (182–3).

In a later work Laclau sought to refine this analysis under the influence of Lash and Urry's account of 'disorganized capitalism' (Lash and Urry 1987; Laclau 1990: 58). This posited the empirical dissolution of the centre around which the intelligibility of the social had hitherto been articulated. Complexity is expressed as a plurality of dislocations that 'increasingly dominate the terrain of an absent structural determination'. In other words, the objectivity of complexity is measured in relation to its determination by an absent centre, or, to say the same thing differently, the absence of a centre is made present as a plurality of dislocations organized around it. The condition of plurality is a nostalgia for the body and in this respect one wonders how it is supposed to differ from the modern 'dissolution of the markers of certainty', except in so far as each plural entity is more prepared to imagine itself as its own centre external to the context in which it enjoys its plurality. In this scenario the subject is dislocation and subject-position is relegated to the level of myth, although this is accompanied by a seven-page elaboration on the necessity of myth as a positive force (61–8) that serves to undermine the possibility of distinguishing between the popular and the democratic. This means that it becomes impossible to distinguish the mythical status of the 'positivist illusion' and the centre around which it is organized from the era of 'complexity' and the dissolution of a centre. At best, we could refer to the randomization of myths, or rather the generalization of the desire to occupy the position that would centre the social. In other words, everyone wants to be universally popular as there is no privileged position that would centre the social and thus provide its objectivity.

This does not eliminate the myth that this can be done. In fact, this becomes a structurally necessary feature. It is the means through which equivalence is maintained. Laclau explains this in the following terms:

Just as gold has the dual function of having its own use value and of embodying the general form of value, the concrete particularity of an institution or social force takes on the function of representing universality itself. (76)

To argue in this manner is simply to explain the necessity of myth by reference to the content of another myth, the magical properties of gold, and to elevate this myth to the level of the necessity of the economy that it grounds and within which it circulates. This logic is extended in the description of the process in which a particular becomes emptied of any concrete content and functions as a surface on which a variety of 'concrete demands' can be inscribed. Through this the particularity in question enjoys a double popularity. It is both place-holder of its own myth of its own popularity and at the same time ground of the popularity of each particularity within the economy that it supports. Universality is displaced on to the circulation of particulars and through this circulation community is constituted as it 'establishes an equivalence between an increasingly wide range of demands' (80). Hence equivalence, or hegemony within postmodernity, is the circulation of the mythical dimension that each particularity has in common, in which a particularity is both the myth of itself and the universality of myth as such through which each particularity is exchanged with every other. Here, being popular simply depends on the manner in which one pragmatically negotiates the commonality of myth or the avoidance of the absence of foundations.

On closer examination we find that in fact this rests on the assumption of the existence of an additional mythical space through which popular myths circulate and on which they depend. It is the myth of exchange itself in which particulars are related through a common currency that acts as a universal equivalent: that is to say, the myth of the objectivity of the economic nature of exchange, of economy as a self-regulating mechanism through which the value of myth circulates. Far from having broken with the essentialism of the economic base on which a superstructure arises, Laclau has displaced the perfection of the economy on to all identifiable instances of the social. [16] At present nothing is more objective than this myth. Even the most violent fluctuations of 'globalization' do not weaken its purchase. In this respect we can assess the status of the universality that arises from this articulation between the circulation of myth and the myth of circulation. According to Balibar no one would dispute that the universality of 'globalization' is real in the sense that interdependence overwhelms independence (1995). Yet it would be surprising if the dynamic of its complexity simply followed without friction, in the manner of a smooth transition. We would agree with Appadurai (1992) that disjuncture is more characteristic than equivalence in this scenario. This arises from the violence of those interventions that seek to implement the smooth running of exchange. In support of this they seek to inscribe a *fictional* universality which is not totalitarian in the manner of something like a univocal world view, but is in fact pluralisitic. In this 'particular identities are relativized and become mediations for the realization of a superior and more abstract goal' (Balibar 1995: 58).

Where then are the dimensions of antagonism and the presence of the political subject to be located? Our answer would be consistent with Laclau and Mouffe's definition of antagonism. Antagonism emerges in those moments when the economy does not correspond to itself, or when the myth of its self-constitution or the autopoietic evolution of its 'complexity' is dislocated. Indeed, Laclau almost goes this far in his recognition that 'more and more areas of social life must become the product of *political* forms of reconstruction and regulation' (81, original emphasis). This is to say that 'complexity' entails the increased politicization of particulars. We would take this further. Antagonism constitutes the presence of power within the terrain on which particulars circulate, or what we would call the pure form of 'political economy' through which the battles around its construction are inscribed. It is through this presence that the political subject enjoys its purchase. At the same time the political subject is not conceived as a particular, nor does it enjoy the status of the universality of exchange in which each particular is measured as each scrambles to obtain its share of the distribution. This is because the political subject is not a thing or a position but a moment or gap between given enunciative possibilities through which any given distribution of identities or classifications is dislocated, including that from which one might speak (Rancière 1995b). Subjectivization is polemicization in so far as it does not seek an identification with the distribution of appearances. However, this should not be confused with those who would refuse their place in the distribution of appearances simply as a means of placing others within a distribution that they alone determine. This simply reproduces the modern political subject in mythical form, stripped of its reference to contingency. It is to a consideration of the democratic practice required to contest this that we now turn. As we shall see, this turns on the issue of the use of universality, and in particular on a confrontation with 'the impossibility of actually achieving freedom *without* equality, or equality *without* liberty' (Balibar 1995: 74) or *equaliberty*.

Notes

1. This is the strategy adopted by Fuss (1989).
2. Kristeva points out that in contemporary society 'the family has ceased to be the basic structure of production and is itself in dissolution' (158).
3. Kristeva's view was echoed by Samuel Brittan's *Capitalism and the Permissive Society*, which appeared in 1973 and was republished in 1988 as *A Restatement of Economic Liberalism*. An award-winning columnist for the *Financial Times*, government economic adviser, Oxbridge fellow and apologist for the free market before the rise of Hayek, Friedman, Thatcher and Reagan, Brittan sought to convert the New Left to the benefits of the market by arguing that 'to the extent that it prevails, competitive capitalism is the biggest single force acting on the side of what it is fashionable to call "permissiveness", but what was once known as personal liberty' (1988: 1). In this Brittan joined the New Left attack on legislation over 'obscene publications' and 'the hysterical and vindictive attitude adopted by so many authority figures towards the problem of drugs' (5). As is well known, as they aged most of the New Left got on board capitalism as soon as it became socially acceptable to do so. Brittan's brother Leon became a Chancellor in Thatcher's government.
4. This is apparent from the famous first paragraph of Rousseau's *The Social Contract*.

   > Man is born free; and everywhere he is in chains. One thinks himself the master of others, and still remains a greater slave than they. How did this change come about? I do not know. What can make it legitimate? That question I think I can answer.

   It is this qualification that announces Rousseau's real intention, which he spectacularly failed to realize.
5. For an account of how contingency in the first sense became actuarial through the refinement of stochastic methods of representation after the emergence of modernity, see Hacking (1975).
6. Mbembe and Roitman (1995) provide a brilliant description of this experience based on fieldwork in postcolonial Cameroon in the early 1990s. They take 'crisis' in two senses: firstly, as 'a constitutive site of particular forms of subjectivity'; and secondly,

as 'the very act of signifying this moment'. Both determine 'specific regimes of subjectivity' or 'pragmatics of subjection' which become normalised and embedded in the everyday. In this case 'crisis' refers to the dislocation of representations of continuous development and wealth creation through which the ruling regime sustained its legitimacy. Due to the effects of global financial governance within which the Cameroonian economy and polity are inscribed, this ceased to function but was not replaced. Hence Cameroonian citizens experienced the crisis tautologically; that is, in terms of the crisis. Accordingly, common experience became inexplicable. Thus:

> The sudden nature of this intrusion is well illustrated by popular expressions: 'The crisis fell on our heads' (*La crise est tombée sur nois têtes*) and 'I've got the crisis' (*J'ai la crise*) . . . the transformations taking place are not necessarily correlated to precise factors and historical referents, even if one is aware that these elements do in fact exist. For lack of these referents, the crisis is exiled to the domain of the inexplicable. (338)

7. For an account of the actual *practice* of practice, one should refer to the inspiring work of de Certeau (1984).
8. In a manner related to the position described here Judith Butler has brilliantly shown, with the aid of a post-deconstructive reading of Austin's theory of Speech Acts, that the presumption of the fullness of enunciation serves to reinstate the (legal) fantasy of subjective self-determination which antagonism reveals. Her paradigmatic example is the belief that gangsta rap, or 'African-American men who sing', is responsible for sexual injury to women, rather than 'the weakening of rights to reproductive freedom and the widespread loss of public assistance' (Butler 1997a: 23).
9. The common sense of Smith's argument is that subject-positions are plural. Nothing is said concerning the plurality of structural positions.
10. In this sense individuals are like Lestat in the Anne Rice novel *Interview with the Vampire*. Lestat has no idea why he is a vampire and his life is devoted to trying to find out why this is the case. Consequently, in order to have a life he must drink the blood of others and thus remains a vampire. The cruel irony is that he is unable to explain to those he converts to vampirism in this way why they too have become vampires.
11. The symptom of this fantasy in Smith's argument is the assertion that individuals are alienated.

12. In fact, Laclau's notion of the 'impossibility of society' is posited through an insistence on returning to the necessity of ideology and mis-recognition. Thus: 'Utopia is the essence of any communication and social practice' (1990 [1983]: 92). In a later work Laclau retreated to the Althusserian 'eternal ideology' position on the basis that this is a strict consequence of the fact that no one can have ultimate and total knowledge (Laclau and Zac 1994). We do not see this as a necessary consequence at all. It would only be relevant in situations where the claim that one can have such knowledge is made politically. Such situations have yet to be specified, although one of these may be the non-reflexive character of the discourse that proposes the necessity of ideology.

13. Copjec gives no justification for this interpretation of Foucault and we very much doubt its accuracy. For Copjec Foucault functions as a phantasmatic other that constitutes psychoanalytic discourse by threatening it, to use the explanatory schema adopted by psychoanalysis to explain the response of those who do not accept the truth of its discourse.

14. For example: 'There is a tragic justice in the fact that the action of the head of the family in stooping to a servant-girl is atoned for by his daughter's self-abasement,' from letter to Fliess, 2 May 1897, 'The Part Played by Servant Girls', quoted in Fuss (1995: 22).

15. In this respect Copjec's account of the Subject coincides exactly with Landry and Maclean's.

16. Here we would agree with Diskin's critique of Laclau on a closely related point, which reiterates the argument made above concerning the coincidence of logic and existence.

> There is simply no foundation in Laclau's *philosophy* for this political conclusion. I believe that, for Laclau, it follows from the 'givenness' of capitalism in his discourse and the presumed universality of the democratic space. He has passed, within the terrain of his own discourse, from the logic of a theoretical argument to programmatic notions, suggesting that the latter can be deduced from the former. What is missing is a reconstructed (nonessentialist) notion of economic life, and this absence allows for Laclau's implicit assertion of a correspondence between historical action and the nature of existence itself. (1994: 143, original emphasis)

Chapter 4

Polemicizing Universals

4.1 The Persistence of Universals

Finally, let us consider polemicization with regard to universals. The debate on postmodernity, notably in the field of cultural studies, made us aware of the political dimension of the universalist claims that legitimated the grand narratives of the Enlightenment. The subsequent criticism of totalizing narratives and the concomitant vindication of particularity threw universals into disrepute. They became suspect of complicity with intellectual traditions that subordinated difference to sameness in the name of History, Reason, Order or what have you. Many saw this as a particularity, the West, representing itself as universal in order to consolidate an economic and political hegemony. The critique of this was not done in the name of the familiar opposition between true and false universality, but in the name of a resistance to universality itself, and to those techniques of representation which derived from it. In other words, resistance was about not being incorporated within the symbolic universe of the powerful as a way of evading this power. The overall effect was to reverse the strategy of the dominant and at the same time avoid making any universalist claims.

One hoped-for result of this reversal was an increased sensibility towards micropolitics, particularity and the right to be different. These themes played a pivotal role in configuring the imaginary of new social movements and identity politics. They also contributed to reposition progressive thought outside its classical Marxist – and state-centred – paradigm of politics. The ethical force behind this derived from the belief that the activation of particularity and difference would guarantee the dignity and self-respect of those marginalized, excluded or oppressed by Western hegemony, and it would do so in a manner that could not be absorbed by the liberal value of toleration, even if toleration was sometimes used against liberalism in order to justify such moves. Thus Western hegemony could be undermined. This belief in the emancipatory potential of difference turned the critique of universalism and the political affirmation of particularity into a programmatic imperative.

More recently, a critique of this view has emerged which reminds us that a mere assertion of difference can easily revert to a cacophony of self-righteous particular groups who have no objective other than the reiteration of their self-righteousness. The defence of otherness then becomes a dialectical inversion of the metaphysics of totality. As Laclau and Mouffe observe, one may start criticizing the 'essentialism of the totality' and end with an equally illegitimate 'essentialism of the elements' (Laclau and Mouffe 1985: 103). This makes the case for the democratic nature of difference difficult to sustain. There is nothing essentially democratic about difference. Rather, its democratic nature has to be produced. This raises serious questions about the chances for democratic ideals and institutions. If the critique of universality, either as a value in itself or as a value which authorizes other values, demonstrated that there is in fact no necessary content to the scope of universality or to those values which it authorizes, then such a critique should be supported and deepened in so far as it prevents the reduction of universality to the level of a reassuring but empty speculation. On the other hand, without the preservation of the question of universality in the very moment of critique, something worse happens. Difference itself is elevated to the level of a flat universal supported by the trivial observation that everything is different. The consequence of this is that difference becomes a matter of indifference. All aspects of relation, and thus of force, power or hierarchy, disappear from the scene, leaving the enunciation of difference bewildered as to why the autonomous self-enclosure which it seeks fails. As we know, the political consequences of this are both comical and terrifying, ranging from ersatz fundamentalism to the violent policing of imaginary boundaries.

This can lend credibility to opportunism under the guise of an effort to assert particular rights. Steel refers to groups that affirm a perceived grievance as a means to perpetuate their status as victims, and thus their claims to collective entitlements (Steel 1992: 49–53). Advocates of a radical view of difference avoid the menace of an imperialist standard of measurement at the expense of a politically dangerous 'hardening of frontiers' between cultural groups (Steel 1992; Gitlin

1993: 172–7; Visker 1993). This is when the essentialism of the elements – or particular groups – settles in, so much so that to 'do the right thing' in this context would mean to evade judgement and intervention to avoid being accused of causing a wrong. This is to take flight in the sentimental value of alterity, thus reifying a dependence upon it, but an ethics of isolation fuelled by fear of guilt puts one in the unenviable position of celebrating impotence as a life-plan. Lyotard is aware that this is not a viable proposition since linkages between groups do occur. He addresses the issue in terms of discursive regimes. The linkage between phrases of heterogeneous regimes is the unavoidable problem of politics – 'to link is necessary; how to link is contingent' (Lyotard 1988: xiii, 29). Politics then addresses the contingency of the link between incommensurables, a point to which we will return shortly. Not surprisingly, he also rules out indifference, in the sense that the conflicts arising from linking – that is, 'differends' – cannot be avoided. The problem is that he poses the question but offers no way out except by stepping out of the problem; if we cannot find 'what can legitimate judgment', he says, then at least we can find 'how to save the honor of thinking' (Lyotard 1988: xii). On the other hand, multiplicity might strengthen the case for a universal criterion, one capable of translating competing and often contested claims – that is to say, total equalization. While there is some truth to this, people like Vattimo are right in criticizing the nostalgic yearning for what he calls 'the reassuring, yet menacing, closure of horizons' (Vattimo 1992: 10–11). By this he means the desire for a strong foundation capable of functioning as a ground or referent for divergent interpretations. For him, as for Lyotard, a multiple world undermines a universal standard. It shatters the belief in a single reality and turns reality into a 'fable' in the Nietzschean sense of the word. A 'measure of measures' would therefore only multiply the differends.

The question of universality lingers none the less. It can be shown at the level of practice because the demotion of universals is not so clear when one observes actual interventions in the name of a politics of difference. Let us examine, for example, what is at stake in the demand for a minimum quota of women in the national executive of conventional democratic political parties, or in their list of candidates for an election. Some parties within the Socialist International, like the PSOE in Spain and the SPD in Germany, have already adopted a quota system. It is presented as a mechanism to redress gender inequality within political parties. At first sight, this claim seems to break with the universalism of classical democratic thought, for it vindicates a special right (a statutory quota) for a particular group (women). It does this, but it does more as well, for advocates of quotas argue the case for a special right in the name of a universal principle, or rather, they pose the right as a means to fulfil a promise of universal political equality undermined, or even denied, by gender discrimination. By invoking a discourse of rights, which is something that transcends their particularity, they situate their claim in a space of political commonality. The sedimented ideas, arguments, principles, discourses and experiences that circulate in this space cannot always be assimilated either to norms and rules or to pure decisionism. In a way, they constitute a corpus of political jurisprudence characteristic of modern liberal-democratic society. While this corpus is itself the subject of distrust and dispute, it also frames exchanges and provides tactical devices to argue for the introduction of changes. Equality and the positive value of participation, for example, are invoked by women groups as a means to negotiate gender equality in positions of leadership – that is, as a means to institute a new measure of participatory parity.

This suggests an analogy with Sraffa's work on neo-Ricardian economics. Instead of the production of commodities by means of commodities, the tactical use of the discourse of rights functions to produce universals by means of a dispute about universals. Dispute is the occasion of this process. The status of dispute, however, is not so easy to determine. In our example, this production consists of a polemic to test the universality of universal equality, and at the same time, of an effort to institute a particular figure (quotas) to enact that universality. To support this we can refer to Young's careful and productive 'critique of the ideal of universal citizenship' (1989). Young recognized that there are tensions in the very meaning of universality when applied to the political sphere, or that universality is internally differentiated. These constitute the distinctions between universality as inclusion and participation of everyone, universality as generality, and universality as equal treatment. One notes that this assumes the unitary nature of political power but, this objection aside, Young succeeds in making a strong case for a practice of citizenship which does not require all citizens to be the same, and which does not relegate difference to the so-called private sphere, as the corpus of modern political thought tends to do. The purpose of this is to undermine a homogenizing and normative dominance exercised by those with power and privilege, and to save those who do not conform from having to become like this in order to be able to express their particular voice. In the 'heterogeneous public' which Young proposes, 'differences are publicly recognized and acknowledged as irreducible, by which I mean that persons from one perspective or history can never completely understand and adopt the point of view of those with other group-based perspective and histories' (258). Basing incommensurability on a self-conscious univocity of the 'one' is perhaps somewhat optimistic.

Yet Young is aware that the simple representation of such perspectives is pointless without a prior commitment to commonality as 'the need and desire to decide together the society's policies fosters communication across those differences.' It is because of this that Young rejects the idea that there is anything essential about differences as they are the contingent outcome of prior conflicts and contestation. The democratic polity is sustained by the principle of its becoming democratic. It is not a stable referent that could be exhaustively described. This allows Young to introduce the mechanism of 'special rights', similar to the notion of quotas above, through which the particularity of universal rights is exposed in order to sustain the universal project of democratic participation. Indeed, Young may well have conceded too much to an optimistic universality when she concludes: 'I do not believe that challenging the ideal of a unified public or the claim that rules should always be formally universal subverts the possibility of making rational normative claims' (274). We would depart from this slightly and suggest 'rational normative claims' are themselves contingently founded and in fact refer to a radically situated process of negotiation and deliberation. It is because of this that we would not use this phrase and we attempt to describe some sort of alternative below which preserves the dimension of conflict.

In the above examples universality and the particular constitute the dispute in a game of exception and rule, yet neither can be reduced to conceptual stability; the rule is, there will always be exceptions. This means that polemicization does not stand under a concept. This does not mean that it is purely empirical either, or that it is alien to the conceptual. Here we could follow Deleuze and Guattari's remarks about the production of concepts. As they rightly point out, 'The first principle of philosophy is that Universals explain nothing but must themselves be explained' (1994: 7). Our focus on the political dimension of concepts entails that we modify the ideal scenario to which this explanation refers. Politically, this does not take place against the assurances of the citified space of the *agon* (Deleuze and Guattari 1994). The common rivalry over the love of the thing which produces commonality, what Deleuze and Guattari refer to as a 'generalized athleticism', is replaced by a no less passionate distrust of the concept and thus, in our terms, of the corpus of political jurisprudence which sustains it. Commonality is brought into question. Concepts are brought into being through dispute. They are not the grounds of dispute.[1]

The existence of the quota system, or of 'special rights', is a contingent outcome of conflicts concerning equality and the means to achieve it. This is how it takes place. The 'filling' of the principle of equality based on quotas is contingent because it could have always been otherwise and can always be dislodged by another filling. In fact there is no reason why equality should be thought only in terms of either quotas or rights. These are simply useful practical devices. Laclau understands what we have called 'production of universals by means of (a dispute about) universals' in terms of the logic of the signifier. A difference – a particular content or claim, an exception – becomes the signifier of an absent fullness on the condition that it prevents such fullness (Laclau 1994). For him there is a necessary non-coincidence between the claim and the universal, between a particular embodiment and the principle of universality as such, in so far as the universal attempts to be exhaustive, which of course is the aim of universality. Indeed, in Laclau's case the semiotic concept of the sign is itself an attempt to constitute universality, while at the same time demonstrating that this is impossible.

This principle of universality requires the event in which it is brought into question. An analogy with Heidegger's lesson of the broken hammer is appropriate here. One only understands what a hammer is when it breaks. This disrupts the routine, taken for granted the status of the tool. This is hardly instrumental, as in its breaking its purpose can be rethought. It ceases to be merely itself. In the case of the social-democratic practice we are considering, a particular group (women) doubles itself and attempts to assume the task of representing both the absence and the possibility of universality (equality) through a specific measure (quotas). The usual notion of equality is thus broken through this double inscription. To the alarm of some, women even appear to cease being merely themselves and assume a dynamic specificity, dislocating conventions of what is appropriate. Put in Laclau's terminology, whether it is seen as an excess of the universal in relation to particular claims, or as the insufficiency of the latter to incarnate fully the universal principle of equality, this non-coincidence opens the field of political contestation for other efforts to hegemonize, or fix, the content of universality differently (Laclau 1994: 174–6).

Contestation introduces a moment of force – and thus of power and hierarchy – in the negotiation of quotas, for advocates of quotas for women attempt to reactivate and dislocate the sedimented forms of political equality and participation despite or against the patriarchal discourses that circulate within the space of commonality of the party. Necessarily, this involves an element of distrust or suspicion. Women simultaneously aim to affirm an identity (a differential 'us women') through confrontation with a male-dominated outside that constitutes women as excluded. Resistance to quotas – contestation by other groups – presupposes that the success of the claim is unlikely to come out of a unanimous decision and that force comes into play. For example, a female electoral constituency within the party or in society at large hangs as a collateral threat to the leadership, and is likely to be exploited to facilitate the political re-entry of the excluded. Yet while a quota aims to redress the exclusion of women from positions of leadership, and thus reconfigure political equality, it also creates a new exclusion by imposing limits to the range of positions available to other groups or individuals within the party. Although the question of the goodness or badness of this exclusion is dependent on the event of its contestation, it nevertheless serves to demonstrate the constitutive impurity of universality. Emphatically, it does not invalidate the legitimacy of quotas as a measure to establish gender equality. We already indicated that the non-coincidence between the measure of equalization and the principle of universal equality is not accidental but necessary. The gap between them opens the political field where polemics and contestation take place. The legitimacy of quotas appears when its acceptance is already secured – that is, when the struggle for quotas has successfully hegemonized the political field and erased (or at least diffused) the memory of the exclusionary violence involved in its institution.[2] This indicates that the negotiation of quotas, of a measure that functions as a means to enact universal political equality, is at the same time a negotiation of the acceptance of that measure. The polemic around gender equality also functions as a means to recreate or reconfigure the space of commonality of the party and the identity of participants. It is a commonality without reconciliation, or rather, one that shows the impossibility of constituting the space of commonality as an indivisible One; the common space of action within the party remains a fissured space, if only because of gender divisions.

The example of quotas illustrates a purely political way of posing universality. Equality appears not as an autonomous referent but as an object of a polemic that also shapes the identity of the parties and the terrain of polemic itself. The strategic pursuit of quotas is also marked by an ambiguity. Equality is sought in the name of a particular group that explicitly wishes to maintain its identity as such – more precisely, which seeks to configure that identity and accentuate its difference from the rest – while it invokes something that transcends its very particularity. What appears to be a purely particular claim is actually contaminated by a reference to an absent term, universality. This reference is how the particularity is enacted. Quotas are presented as a means to address a wrong, the denial of full equality for women, with the purpose of redressing the wrong by fulfilling universal political equality. The latter remains the guiding thread of the pursuit of quotas even, and especially, as the contours of equality are transformed through it. Hence the ambiguity of particularity, which instead of an autonomous, self-contained difference, is always already impure by definition, constitutively indebted to something other than particularity.

This ambiguity is interesting for us in that it suggests that the demotion of universality is a moot point, at least from a practical standpoint. However, our objective here is not only to prove the practical import of universals for politics but also to think how they may be theorized within an afoundational terrain. This task cannot be reduced to the banal observation that universals cannot conform to the caricature of absolute, all-encompassing referents intent on subjugating difference in the name of sameness. Neither does it consist of finding the right balance between two essentialisms, of the totality and of the elements, or of proposing an intermediate notion to reconcile universality and particularity. Instead, it can be formulated as an enquiry about what Rancière calls 'measures of incommensurables' or, alternatively, what we describe as the status of referents for contested claims when multiplicity is a fact and the substance of community or ground of dissent is in question – that is, when a certain objectivity or hegemony is at stake and polemics is in the order of the day.

Taking on the question of universality will enable us to propose a notion of a contingent and constitutively 'impure' universal that arises in scenarios of dispute between claimants, and show how the polemic about universals simultaneously shapes the space of that polemic as a place of division. In other words, we will see that both the political purchase of universals and the space of commonality arise in and through polemicization. The discussion will focus on equality, or rather, on measures of equality or of equalization for contested claims. These measures, however, are not necessarily identical to equality as a universal value. There is no need to invoke universal equality when a political party configures its list of candidates to reflect a plural constituency of women, blacks, immigrants and so on. This can be done for purely pragmatic reasons, either to accommodate the demands of various organized groups within the party or to present a more diverse electoral ticket to appeal to an equally diverse mass of voters. Yet there is none the less a significant conceptual overlap between equalization and equality when the emphasis falls on the *measure*, for this fosters a double connection between them: firstly, because in both cases there is a dispute that revolves around the status of the referent, so that whatever stands for universality as a value and equalization as a measure emerges in an essentially impure way; and secondly, because the question of universality comes into play in measures of equalization when equality breaks down or is put into question and there is a polemic about the meaning of equality. This would be the case when the argument for a measure, as in the example of women quotas in positions of leadership of political parties, appeals to a discourse of rights and to the principle of equality to underline the absence of full political equality. So when we refer to quotas or any other measure of equalization we are actually interested in situations where these measures are proposed as means to realize universality and where the actual universality of universals is at stake, caught up in polemic contests to determine their political purchase.

4.2 The Pragmatics of the Referent

The referent is not of the order of a subjective determination of objectivity, of playing the game of representing a particular difference as universal. Modernity constrained itself by defaulting to this option and the various postmodern critiques have shown that this is no longer viable. Neither is the referent a question of some mysterious inter-subjectivity, and even less one of a retreat into the insulated differences of 'the new sovereignties', as it is at this level that it is easiest to discover an underlying commonality. Rather, the answer lies in the contingent nature of the referent itself, or the nature of the relation between the same and its contingency.[3] This relation is the in-between through which politics is possible.

To argue this we must show how equivalence and difference can be maintained without the presumption of totality that determines their relation. The question that follows for us is: if political equality is always conceived of as *equalization*, a term that allows us to maintain differences among those who are equalized, what is the status of that which equalizes – of the referent that stands as a *measure* of equalization – within a terrain that cannot be dominated by the purity of equality or difference? What especially concerns us is what may happen in cases of conflict between measures of equalization. We see three possible scenarios. In one a measure replaces another, in the form of a substitution, as something like a 'measure of measures' emerges to enable the conversion. We have seen how this only multiplies conflicts. In another scenario relativism forecloses the likelihood of measuring and any general authoritative criterion is distrusted. Lyotard's notion of the differend applies to this case, as a wrong occurs if the general law of incommensurability is broached, although no particular reason is given as to why this injunction should be observed.[4] Finally, in a third scenario the notion of measure itself loses its referential independence and cannot be taken for granted. Our argument will support the latter.

One might ask whether this option invalidates universality as a legitimate topic of enquiry. This all depends on the status of universals and their relation to differences. This can be illustrated with an example drawn from the practices of exchange in contemporary currency markets. Until 1971, setting the exchange rate between different national currencies was a rather straightforward procedure thanks to the dollar-gold standard. The Bretton Woods agreements of 1944 set a system of fixed exchange rate whereby the value of a currency was fixed against gold. The US dollar became the universal measure in this system mainly because of the reassurance provided by the dollar's convertibility to gold. At the time, the US Federal Reserve Bank held an estimated eighty per cent of the total world gold reserves. It used it to back the dollar by guaranteeing that any central bank holding US currency could convert it into gold on demand at a fixed price of thirty-five dollars an ounce. The cracks in this arrangement became apparent in the late 1960s when de Gaulle took a political decision, doubtless in defence of national honour, and demanded that American debts to France be paid in gold, not dollars. He took advantage of the trick whereby money signifies value and challenged money to its face, as it were. If gold was to be the universal measure of value there was no reason why it should be the exclusive property of one of the participants of international trade. Hence, de Gaulle got rid of the middleman and eliminated the illusion of a particular difference, the dollar, representing itself as a universal measure of equivalence. The stock of gold held at Fort Knox haemorrhaged and in 1971 the Nixon administration suspended the convertibility of the dollar in recognition of the collapse of the gold standard and of Bretton Woods. The market was left without a referential unit of measure to determine the exchange rate or purchasing power of one currency in relation to another. Gold could no longer play the role of universal mediator of equivalence. Consequently, one can no longer read off relations of equivalence and difference from this form.

The absence of a fixed standard did not prevent the market from setting the value of currencies. It only compelled it to seek a different mechanism to do so. Capital realized that there was no major disadvantage in relying on the conventional nature of exchange. In this respect capital becomes a form of semiotics (Goux 1990; Shapiro 1993). After 1971, the fixed-rate regime was replaced with a flexible-rate system where currencies were free to 'float' against one another. This meant that their individual strengths and weaknesses did not always spread evenly. Parity was not uniformly determined; the mark could go up against the pound but lose ground against the yen or the dollar, the franc could gain ground against the dollar but lose it in relation to the yen, and so on. The new setting introduced asymmetry, in the sense of a 'combined and uneven development' of exchange rates, as well as contingency in the value of national currencies. It was also more complex, due both to the variety of criteria involved in the calculation of currency values and the need to attune strategic calculation to the shifting weight of each criterion. Money became increasingly abstract and increasingly volatile (Leyshon and Thrift 1997). No longer simply a medium of exchange, money itself became exchangeable and started to act like other commodities. Here we enter the period of what is sometimes optimistically referred to as 'late capitalism' or 'disorganized capitalism' (Offe 1985; Lash and Urry 1987).[5] Money circulates as a sign of itself, but its referent is constantly transformed; or, to be more precise, the speed of oscillation between the referential and self-referential aspects of money increases. As we know, this sort of activity is celebrated in films like *Wall Street* and *Bonfire of the Vanities*. European sociologists refer to it in terms of the emergence of 'risk society'. Profit becomes dependent on the slowness of circulation.

What positive political benefits can be derived from such a state of affairs? There are two. Firstly, we should notice that this example avoids positing both an absolute ground and pure particularity. Equivalence is not governed by a single, fixed norm, a 'measure of measures' like the dollar-gold standard. It does not rest on the arbitrary, 'subjective' decision of each central bank either. Instead, it is constructed through the interplay of various criteria. These include the relative strength of each country's economy, the effects of political events like wars or elections, people's expectations about the impact of monetary and fiscal policy, fluctuations in the rate of interest, and speculative operations of currency brokers and central banks. Parity, then, is being produced and transformed continually through the interplay of these criteria in the language game of exchange markets. In fact, if this implicit analogy with Wittgenstein's theory of language games is to be accurate, we can say that the players don't know how big the board is and that the rules are part of the game. Equivalence is no longer based on an autonomous referent outside the process of exchange, but a fluctuating difference set in an ongoing process of negotiating exchange rates. This process creates both the measure of parity, as a fluctuating equivalence between different currencies, and the validity of the measure among the players in the language game of currencies. Difference, or the exchange rate between currencies, is a contingent outcome of strategic calculations, decisions and initiatives, whether concerning the weight assigned to each criterion or the timing of the decisions. It takes place under conditions of incomplete information and in the face of conflicting efforts of different monetary authorities and speculators to weaken or strengthen a particular currency. On the one hand, this indicates that the negotiation of parity involves an uncertainty that cannot be dispelled; it sets the temporary purchasing power of currencies measured against each other, which can neither presuppose nor guarantee that the standing of all players and all currencies will be improved. On the other hand, at each moment a difference in exchange rates is simultaneously an equivalence, but both can never be absolutely equivalent or absolutely different as these distinctions are dependent on their relations with the circumstances in which this event 'takes place'.

Secondly, this does not correspond to any particular position of articulation. Here we would emphasize that our concern is with *articulatory practices*, although not in the sense that this presents the political domain with an emptiness waiting to be filled. Instead, what is produced in this encounter is a universal that is neither true nor false. Rather, it is pragmatic in the sense of *pragmata* or things of the world. Moreover, the parties to the exchange are transformed through it. This is obviously the case in currency exchange but an even sexier example has recently come to light. In her book *Becoming-Woman* Camilla Griggers examines the current position of the lesbian considered as a force in the contemporary American cultural-political economy. Griggers uses the ontology of Deleuze and Guattari to undertake a 'materialist critique of lesbianism itself' (1997: 52). Not surprisingly, the position of the lesbian is a curious one, comprising both the *striated* space of the state-military-industrial-pharma-prosthetic complex, and the *smooth* space of the joy-lines of flight-glamour-speed complex. Thus: 'lesbians are becoming nomad run-aways *and* becoming state *at the same time*' (51, original emphasis). They want both to kill their parents and to be parents. No one intended this. The political stakes are greatest at the moment in which *majoritarian* becomes *minoritarian* – that is to say, when the existence of equivalence and difference is most in question through an equalization of forces. Griggers is careful to point out that this results in multiple conflicts that are not totalizable because of the differences presented by the tasks to be done in each case. There is no real universal, only the conflict of measures of equalization. We would say that this takes place through the *pragmata* of universals.

4.3 Deliberation and Confrontation

Let us look into these measures in the actual polemic concerning equalization, which means that we must leave aside an external referent and locate the question in the context of this experience. In this we are attempting to give form to the event, and thus we raise the question of the experience of temporality, movement in its most general sense. This is combined with the constitutive status of divisions and of conflicts arising from those divisions, such that whatever unity exists is only a temporary suspension of a division that can be reactivated again but also lead to new divisions. This 'positive onto-political interpretation' is not new. Rancière traces it to Aristotle, for whom politics must address the coexistence of two irreconcilable elements in the city, the rich and the poor, 'ever virtually at war' with one another (Rancière 1995b: 12–13; 1995c: 95–6, 98).[6] It is also a central premise of political modernity, at least from Hobbes onward; order is a response to, and arises from, an original division. Derrida himself – in a tone that pitches his argument along the lines of

Nietzsche in *The Will to Power* – observes that conventions and institutions are stabilizations of something irreducibly unstable and chaotic (Derrida 1996: 82–3). They can domesticate the play of forces but no domestication manages to eradicate the subversive or disruptive effects of that play. For Derrida this irreducible chaos opens up a chance – which is also a risk – to destabilize and change any existing stabilization. At the same time it explains why politics exists and ethics is possible. As we will see shortly, if stability were natural, or at least final, we would inhabit an algorithmic world where there would be room for administration, but not for ethics or politics.

The ontopolitical condition of division, which fuels the interplay between order and disruption, also affects the standing of the contestants. Their relation does not remain untouched by the conflicts they enter, if only because they become a function of the play of delimitation between an inside and an outside, and not merely subjects antecedent to that play. As in the example of quotas, and in questions concerning order or objectivity generally, relations of opposition both configure and reconfigure the identity of – and the modes of solidarity among – the intervening parties. Let us insist on this point. The term 'division' indicates an ontopolitical condition through the fact that something is divided. The violence this implies is not necessarily reducible to a mere act of discrimination that stands as a sign of the breakdown of equality. It also forges further links. Derrida even assigns a constructive role to exclusionary violence that re-enters as a supplement or possible 'constitutive outside' of the unity or identity of an object. Staten explains that this notion refers to an outside that is necessary for the constitution of the phenomenon in its as-such – that is, an outside that functions as a condition of possibility of the inside (Staten 1984: 16–19).

Importantly, less direct modes of re-entry of the constitutive outside occur when the formal recognition of the adversary is absent. We are thinking of displaced others, of the re-entry of political others in parallax. During the dictatorial rule of Stroessner and his Colorado Party in Paraguay, only legal and largely compliant parliamentary parties were recognized as legitimate opposition. The core opposition of extra-parliamentary parties and movements was formally excluded from the political sphere and denied the status of legitimate adversaries. They were branded as illegal political formations and dealt with through criminal laws – law 209, 'Of Defence of Public Peace and Freedom of Persons', and law 294, 'Of Defence of Democracy'. Yet throughout Stroessner's rule, the efforts of the government, the police, the courts, the official media and the Colorado Party were directed against the extra-parliamentary opposition. That is, excluding the latter from the institutional space of politics did not prevent its re-entry as a political adversary. It only led to a confrontation in parallax, for this excluded opposition still functioned as a constitutive outside of the government. It also proved that confrontation – or for that matter, a process of negotiation – partly configures and modifies the identity of the participants. As Bill Clinton confided several months after his inauguration as President of the United States: 'The painful lesson is that you define yourself by who you fight' (Woodward 1995: 16).[7] In part, this shows that within this fight – which risks the dissolution of the distinction between equality and difference – a space of deliberation opens up. The relation between forces and points of articulation is weakened, in so far as there is no natural necessary relation between these terms. Post-Heideggerian philosophers sometimes refer to this process as the 'decline of ontology'.

Argumentative engagement is important for various reasons. The measure of equality is not something waiting to be uncovered through persistent intellectual endeavour. Neither can it be a task left to one of the claimants, unless we are thinking of a case where one group sets the meaning of a measure that is voluntarily accepted by the others. This is less likely to happen in situations where it really counts – where there is conflict between claimants. One could argue that the government, or any strong claimant, might resort to a unilateral imposition of the measure, which presupposes that it has resources to reduce the opposition, or the adversary generally, to a subordinate place. This is a purely political decision. Yet even if they do, mere imposition generates obedience without moral obligation. It may suppress conflict for a while, but also foster resentment, which ultimately induces rather than suspends conflict around the legitimacy of the measure. The relation between force and identification becomes stronger. The same applies *within* a particular group of claimants like a political party, an ethnic community or a religious organization, which are all cases of particularity within the wider political community.

There is another reason for deliberation. We have seen that the example of currency rates discussed above portrays equivalence as the negotiation of a fluctuating equilibrium in a contested environment. We want to maintain this example as a paradigmatic case that illustrates the construction of equivalence without appealing to an external, autonomous referent. Yet the passage from exchange markets to more political language games is not straightforward and requires an adjustment. Politics modifies the status that negotiation and contestation enjoyed in currency markets. Unlike a political dispute, parity between currencies takes place in a system that needs no argumentative efforts to ground the various moments in its fluctuating equilibrium. There is no polemic in currency markets, so we need to translate the example of the equivalence of currencies into a political case of confrontation about equality and equalization. To paraphrase Lyotard, in the case of politics the 'reality' of equality and of what stands for the measure of equality has to be demonstrated – that is, argued and presented as a case in order to become a state of the referent for claims among claimants (Lyotard 1988: 23, 16).

This is another way of referring to the polemic dimension of equality and whatever stands for a measure of equalization, a point that is posed unambiguously in Rancière's recent work when he links universality with polemic. For him universality is neither the place of a ground or an ideal, nor the *eidos* of the community to which particular situations are opposed (1995b; see also 1995a and 1995c). Instead, he conceives it primarily as a logical operator that exists only to the extent that it is enacted. One might appeal to Man, Human Beings, equality or citizenship, he says, yet universality is not in those concepts but in the polemical verification of what follows from ideas such as citizenship, equality before the law and so on. Hence the political dimension of universality, the fact that the latter is the effect of a practice that puts universals to the test by singularizing them in a dispute that raises the question of knowing in what they are 'truly' universal and in what they are power. Their 'truth' does not derive from a ground; it can only be a contingent outcome of struggles and negotiations. As he put it, the truth of a universal is a *topos*, a discursive and practical construction; it is the effect of an argumentative plot that simultaneously constructs the perceptible space of argumentation. The latter does not presuppose agreement, since Rancière maintains that the parties in a dialogue are irreconcilable; they can hear one another without necessarily agreeing with each other. This argumentative plot is the heart of polemics.

Argumentation, or deliberation, should not be seen as a way to uncover a common standard or referent external to polemic, or as an ideal speech situation seeking to determine the truth of a claim, or as a formal attempt to derive the validity of a claim from a set of premises, or as a means to reconcile a divided community. The first point – the rejection of an autonomous, indisputable referent – was already raised in the example about the contingency of exchange rates between currencies. The referent is precisely what is at stake in a polemic. Lefort reinforces this view when he invokes his well-known thesis concerning the dissolution of markers of certainty in democratic orders, which in fact amounts to an explicit acknowledgement of the contingency of order:

> The institution of democracy came by the rejection of any ultimate standpoint . . . The demand for legitimization imposes itself in the very moment of action and thought. Men [sic] are put to the task of interpreting events, conducts and institutions without being able to have recourse to the authority of a grand judge . . . . In other terms, the world presents itself thus from the vantage point of each unique locus. Impossible to encompass, it nevertheless requires the debate about what is legitimate and what is not as well as, in each individual, a ceaseless effort at judgment. (Lefort 1990: 9–10)

This means that in democratic orders people do not simply reflect the pre-existing norms, for there is a non-coincidence of the inscription and the instituted meaning of that which is inscribed (Ferry 1990: 74). This reiterates our point about the contingency of objectivity: deliberation does not seek to uncover the essence of the referent but to establish its status: that is, the instituted meaning of the inscribed. This concerns the status of the corpus of political jurisprudence, something we will discuss later in connection with undecidability.

Perelman and Manin address the other two points by dissociating argumentation from truth and logical necessity (Perelman 1971; Manin 1987). Perelman links argumentation to practical reasoning. Like legal reasoning, it refers to situations where people seek to justify their opinions or choices by persuading the audience that is being addressed – in other words, by means of rhetoric. Manin, following Perelman, and Aristotle before him, maintains that notions of true and false are inappropriate to describe either the propositions or the final outcome of political controversies. The parties involved in polemical deliberation aim to defend their positions and refute those of their opponents. Their propositions can be stronger or weaker, and the arguments more or less successful in eliciting approval, but little else. In practical reasoning, Perelman says, arguments 'are never conclusive as are formally correct deductions', while Manin states that 'whatever the force of an argumentation, its conclusion is never strictly necessary' (Perelman 1971: 147; Manin 1987: 353). That is why deliberation is in principle controversial and its outcome uncertain.

Similarly it would be a mistake to assume that the argumentation or deliberation that goes on in a polemic is *mere* rhetoric. At the philosophical level Rancière strongly objects to this view and argues that the irreconcilability of the parties antedates any specific dispute (1995c: 97, 102–4). This merely reinforces the ontopolitical condition of division mentioned earlier. For him deliberation is not a means to reach consensus but a way to address a grievance. In democratic dialogue the parties hear one another but do not agree with one another – at least in the sense of a compromise between interests or the formation of a common will. Their dialogue is that of a divided community whose divisions – like the division between rich and poor – are present throughout the process of deliberation and remain even if there is agreement and the grievance is 'settled'. 'Grievance', he says, 'is the true measure of otherness, the thing that unites interlocutors while simultaneously keeping them at a distance from each other.' In other words, difference is located within the same. So the interlocutors in a polemic are not 'partners', and the wrong that gives rise to their dispute is addressed without necessarily getting righted because the 'what' of dispute – precisely, the *pragmata* – is constantly being transformed. In this sense deliberation, as a mode of communication within a divided community – or, alternatively, within a community united by incompletion – resembles a Nietzschean war of interpretations, something that Connolly discusses in ethical terms as 'agonistic respect' (Connolly 1991: 166–7). What is at stake is the status of objectivity – the conformation of both the space of polemic and the referent for the contenders; and, as in any war, force is a constitutive element of the communication between the parties.

That is why argumentation should not be confused with a purely non-violent exchange between equals. From different perspectives Lefort and Fraser challenge the belief that speech is the sole medium of persuasion and that it cannot transmit inequality of power (Lefort 1988: 53–4; Fraser 1992: 119–20). Argumentation is marked by the asymmetry of the intervening parts, if only because of the unequal distribution of speech resources such as rhetorical skills or cultural proficiency. These strengthen the position of those who can master them and reveal that deliberation is not only a matter of rational persuasion, that force and power also intervene in communications between antagonistic parts. Laclau takes this further when he points out that persuasion itself includes an element of violence or force. It is there, he says, when we try to convince someone to change his or her beliefs through purely argumentative means, for this change involves the modification of the person's initial beliefs (Laclau 1991: 89–92).

While persuasion or rhetorical expertise might be seen as an implicit, or even a relatively benign manifestation of force and power, the latter become more visible when the contestants summon non-deliberative – but perfectly democratic – means to engage their counterparts and press for a claim: for example, when they appeal to their institutional positions of authority; when they enter into alliances with other groups; when they use – or threaten to use – their capacity of disruption through demonstrations, strikes, pickets or legal action, and so on. Force is also present in everyday deliberative processes when the majority is invoked to deal with an impasse without resorting to physical violence. The decisionistic force of the majority principle imposes itself when conflicts cannot be resolved through confrontation and negotiation between groups (Manin 1987: 360–61). This measure of force puts a limit to argumentation, even though its enactment is doubly constrained: firstly, by the need to contemplate the legitimacy of the deliberative process that led to the formation of the majority and its assertion of a decision; and secondly, because minorities are likely to persist despite and beyond any majority principle.

The willingness to use these resources indicates several things; firstly, that force is not an accident that befalls argumentation. It is in fact part of the structure of possibility of deliberation as such. Secondly, something is compromised in the polemic around equalization – that is, the communication involved in argumentation includes the possibility of a partial realization of claims. Agreement about a measure of equalization is compatible with a loss that need not be spread evenly among the claimants. Finally, and consequently, negotiation, as in the example of parity between currencies, sets limits to the purity of measures of equalization.

Let us look at this notion of limits. Is the idea of equivalence initially unbound and only later becomes limited through negotiation within a polemic? Clearly not, for the compromise arising from a negotiation is only a second-order limit. One is already present in the ontopolitical claim that assigns a constitutive status to division. We have seen that this division entails a distinction and exclusion, and therefore a frontier and a limit to equality. The second limit functions as a supplement of the initial one. It is a political limit. We mentioned earlier that a division could be reactivated because unity is only a temporary suspension of divisions. Equality, as a contingent outcome of conflicts and strategic calculation, is a sedimented moment in a fluctuating equilibrium. The claimants contest each other's claims in a political negotiation where some attempt to reactivate the sedimented or hegemonic forms of equality to negotiate another equilibrium, while others might try to maintain an existing state of affairs. As in any negotiation, the parties end up granting concessions – whether willingly or not – in the pursuit of their claims. They introduce limits to their initial claims and hence accept some degree of loss. If there is no concession, there is no negotiation either. There might be a zero-sum game, where maximalist demands set the stage for greater exclusion, or pure war, where contenders seek their mutual annihilation as a matter of policy. Short of these situations, the type of exclusion involved in a political negotiation does not cancel out the possibility of validating agreements concerning equality. On the one hand, this dissociates the measure of equality from an absolute notion of universality that is both timeless and impervious to context. On the other hand, it shows that agreement does not require unanimity or, as Manin maintains, that the deliberative process or negotiation itself plays a major role in establishing the legitimacy of a political outcome (Manin 1987: 351–2, 359, 364). This weakens the case for the idea of unbound equality and renders the measure of equality an impure category, different both from pure identity and pure equality.

4.4 Undecidability and the Impurity of Universals

This constitutive impurity of measures puts into question the universality of universals. We may recall how this works in the deliberative process. Argumentation distances itself from the idea of reconciliation, does not presuppose an ideal speech situation and takes for granted that in a divided community 'objectivity' arises from wars of interpretation where force is present. It seeks to establish the instituted meaning of the inscribed – in this case, of the referent as a *measure* of equality. The contestable nature of the inscribed indicates that no inscription can achieve the status of a pure presence – that is, that the referent is not prior or external to the process of deliberation. It is caught up in that process and is produced by it, so that the universality of the referent is confronted by a certain limit that announces its impurity. The argument about impurity, however, rested mostly on references to argumentation within a polemic, which in a way is primarily a condition of possibility for the contingency of equality. Now we should move on to discuss this essential impurity in the very structure of the referent. For this we will introduce Derrida's notion of undecidability.

Polemicization reveals the undecidable status of decisions concerning norms generally. Some pre-existing rules or norms like those governing citizenship and the legal equality of participants, together with discourses, arguments and experiences concerning those norms, inform the strategic calculation of claimants. This is what we mean by a corpus of political jurisprudence. Yet these rules do not remain unaffected by the conflict between claimants. Contestation involves contrasting interpretations about the validity and the meaning of the rules themselves. Interpretation involves something more than a simple application of pre-existing rules. It is an attempt to conserve and to reinvent the rules simultaneously, which is another way of saying that rules are inserted in language games whereby every use is also a reformulation (Wittgenstein); or, as Derrida would have it, that rules are *iterable* – that is, that they are marks whose 'citability' or repetition involves a paradoxical self-identity. Rules retain their identity (sameness) while they are redescribed (altered) (Derrida 1988: 8–10). If iterability is part of the structure of possibilities of rules, then there is an element of uncertainty concerning the status of their identity at a given moment – that is, concerning the validity of an interpretation. Indeed, interpretation cannot be fully grounded on pre-existing rules because it involves some degree of reinstitution of those rules. This creates a gap between the rules we follow and the continual process of redescription involved in their actualization. It is here, in this gap, that Derrida locates what he calls the 'undecidability' faced by every free decision. It is here, too, that Rancière's reference to the polemic contest about the status of universals opens up the field of political hermeneutics – of wars of interpretation. As in the case of the absent community we will present shortly, this polemic contest, and in fact politics, can only arise because of this gap or 'in-between' where both the status of rules and the gap itself as a ground of dissent are at stake.

Derrida's reasoning concerning undecidability revolves around the question of justice (Derrida 1992). While it deconstructs the relation between legal norms and juridical decisions, undecidability is not only about the judge who faces the singular case. What he calls 'the ordeal of the undecidable' is an ontopolitical claim; undecidability configures the topic of the decision as soon as one concedes that there is no transcendental signified or indisputable ground to settle a polemic among claimants. In this sense undecidability is not confined only to justice and legal norms but applies to polemics generally. The situation he poses is as follows: if a rule necessarily adopts a general form, but an act of justice must address the singularity of the unique situation, can an action be *legal* and also *just*?

> To be just [says Derrida] the decision of the judge, for example, must not only follow a rule of law or a general law but must also assume it, approve it, confirm its value, by a reinstituting act of interpretation, as if ultimately nothing previously existed of the law, as if the judge himself invented the law in every case. No exercise of justice as law can be just unless there is a 'fresh judgment'. (1992: 23)

This situation presents us with justice as the experience of an aporia:[8] the decision must follow a rule and at the same time cannot be merely derived from that rule. Justice involves an excess vis-à-vis calculation and the law, for the decision must introduce a fresh judgement whereby the (legal) norm is virtually reinvented. That is why he says that a decision is free only when it faces up to the ordeal of the undecidable, the ordeal of finding an appropriate passage where there is none at hand.

> The undecidable is not merely the oscillation or tension between two decisions; it is the experience of that which, though heterogeneous, foreign to the order of the calculable and the rule, is still obliged . . . to give itself up to the impossible decision, while taking account of laws and rules. (1992: 24)

Consequently, the notion of decision cannot be embodied by a particular political actor in its enunciation. While this was the internal limit of the *polemology* behind Schmitt's concept of the 'political' (Schmitt 1996 [1932]), we should first mention the uncanny resemblance between his position and Derrida's. (For a critique of Schmitt's polemology see Chapter 2 of this book and Derrida 1997.) He also criticizes the longing for a normative dimension capable of choosing or deciding for us, for he realizes that every juridical decision is lodged between the general norm and the singular case. Schmitt conceives decisions as 'unruly practices', in the sense that the singularity of the concrete juridical decision cannot be fully derived from the content of the norms (Schmitt 1985 [1922, 1934]: 16–35). Otherwise there would be no space for contingency, since decisions would be replaced by the self-realization of norms. The legal interest for decisions, he says, 'is derived from the necessity of judging a concrete fact concretely even though what is given as a standard for the judgement is only a legal principle in its general universality' (1985: 31). The Schmittian

unruliness introduces the 'other' of pure normativity. Following
Hobbes, he claims that *auctoritas, non veritas facit legem* (power
rather than reason creates law), which means, as we will see later, that
force, or violence, is embedded in the structure of the law and of other
measures of equality when these aim to enact universality. Schmitt
also invokes the idea of *auctoritatis interpositio* – that is, the intervention of the judge, of that which stands between the norm and its
application – to remind us that the juridical decision functions as a
constitutive supplement of the norm. 'Every concrete juristic decision',
he says, 'contains a moment of indifference from the perspective of
content, because the juristic deduction is not traceable in the last detail
to its premises and because the circumstance that requires a decision
remains an independently determining moment' (1985: 30). The
mediation of the decision, which is also the moment of interpretation,
is not accidental but ineradicable. It is an 'in-between' that is both the
site and the matter of dispute.

As in Derrida's case of undecidability, for Schmitt the aporetic
nature of the decision stems from its location between the norm and a
certain indifference to its content; and as for Derrida, too, the
unruliness of decisions is only partial, for he does not dissociate them
from norms altogether. So neither Derrida nor Schmitt pretends to
replace the relativism of purely normative approaches by an equally
illegitimate practical relativism of the decision-maker. Otherwise they
would have to endorse a conservative stance that reduces the problem
of decision to the dictate of authorities – that is, they would have to
introduce a transcendental signified that short-circuits both undecidability and decisionism. Admittedly, Schmitt does refer to a sovereign
decision; he would like it to be a prerogative of the state and thus
reveals a conservative purpose. However, he partly undermines this by
claiming that sovereignty resides in whoever can decide on the
singularity of the exceptional situation – be it a state, a political party
or what have you. In this way contingency contaminates the locus of
the decision, as this place cannot be occupied a priori by a unique,
predetermined agent.

Derrida's refusal to reduce the question of undecidability to a mere
decision of authority, judicial or other, is more subversive in that he
opens a second modality of the aporia of the undecidable. He calls it
the essential ghost of undecidability that is lodged in every decision,
the effect of which is to deconstruct any semblance of fullness of the
justice of a decision, and by implication, prevents the full presence of
the agent that decides. He says:

Once the ordeal of the undecidable is passed (if that is possible), the decision has again followed a rule or given itself a rule, invented it or reinvented, reaffirmed it, it is no longer *presently* just, fully just. There is apparently no moment in which a decision can be called presently and fully just: either it has not yet been made according to a rule, and nothing allows us to call it just, or it has already followed a rule – whether received, confirmed, conserved or reinvented – which in its turn is not absolutely guaranteed by anything; and moreover, if it were guaranteed, the decision would be reduced to calculation and we couldn't call it just. (1992: 24)[9]

Hence his recourse to the notion of *hauntology*, or of the presence of enunciation in time (Derrida 1995). The ghost of the undecidable hangs over every decision in the form of a continual postponement or non-coincidence of the just decision with itself, or rather, to use Derrida's expression, this ghost forces us to conceive justice as 'justice to come' (*à-venir*), as an ethical opening toward the *à-venir* (1992: 27). The *à-venir* of justice is not a Kantian regulative Idea that provides us with a horizon for action. This is not because Derrida dismisses it altogether, but because he believes that such horizon functions as a form of closure in that it is a backdrop against which one can see what is coming (1994b: 50). Instead he conceives the *à-venir* as a 'punctured horizon', an expression that accounts for undecidability and opens up the possibility for what he calls 'the chance of the event and the condition of history'. That is why the idea of a justice to come might be Derrida's way of saying that justice is to be thought as an event along the lines of *différance*: always deferred and at the same time different from itself.

It would be a mistake to think that a promise whose arrival is continually postponed confines justice to the non-place of utopia, or that it condemns us to resignation or pessimism – that is, to conceive justice as impossibility. Neither should we assume that if free decisions do not merely follow rules, then any decision can lay claim to justice and be accepted as just. Derrida sees the promise in its performative dimension; it is an event that takes place here and now in the moment of uttering the promise, which involves a commitment to justice even if the promise is not kept (1996: 81–2). He illustrates this when he speaks of 'democracy to come'. This is not the same as a future democracy, and even less a guarantee that tomorrow it will be realized. The 'to come' of democracy – or of justice, equality or even community – refers to a performative promise that brings forth an engagement with and for democracy. So there is neither resignation nor utopia in the promise or 'to come'; democracy, or justice, is already happening in and through the promise. Similarly, not all decisions can be accepted as just because of the constitutive deferral of justice, what Derrida calls the spectrality that haunts the plenitude of a just decision – that is, the ghost of the undecidable that is lodged in every decision, but also because the undecidability of justice exposes the chances of 'good' calculations as well as 'bad' or 'perverse' ones. If this is so, undecidability cannot serve as an alibi for staying out of what he describes as 'juridico-political battles'. On the contrary, given the possibility of undesirable calculations, Derrida stresses that 'incalculable justice *requires* us to calculate,' which is why he speaks of an ethical opening toward the *à-venir*. It is also why the *à-venir* cannot be occupied by a subject, spoken directly as a statement or enunciation, and this is the case precisely because it 'comes out of one's mouth'. What comes out can never be fully determined by an intention or calculation. Its force cannot be calibrated precisely, even when one says nothing. Yet it is that which all vocalizations are subject to in so far as they indicate the wish or compulsion to be responsible for what is said. One chances one's words. This is the enunciation of incompletion, the always more to be said of community.

This allows us to clarify the ethical dimension of the event. The world has no innate structure, no natural order; it does not run on automatic pilot and is given to us without a blueprint of how to run it ourselves. Like it or not, we have modernity to thank for this. Indeed, it is precisely because there are no secure foundations that life has to be lived in some way other than by reference to them. That is where ethics comes in.

> The fact that must constitute the point of departure for any discourse on ethics [says Agamben] is that there is no essence, no historical or spiritual vocation, no biological destiny that humans must enact or realize. This is the only reason why something like an ethics can exist, because it is clear that if humans were or had to be this or that substance, this or that destiny, no ethical experience would be possible – there would only be tasks to be done. (Agamben 1993: 43; see also Nancy 1997: 131)

So the ethical moment – a call for engagement – comes into play precisely because justice to come has the status of an event, of that which exceeds laws and calculation. Without the possibility of the event, we would have to assume an algorithmic world where undecidability is cancelled out and ethics is redundant. We are drawn into 'juridico-political battles' because justice is not an effect of self-realizing norms, structures, codes and so on. Thus for Derrida undecidability is actually a call for engagement and taking a risk to deal with the decision concerning what is just, or what stands for justice once the ordeal of the undecidable has been confronted and 'passed'. Ethico-political decisions concerning justice, but also equality, democracy or what have you, turn out to be an interminable traversing of the experience of undecidability (Derrida 1996: 85–6). In other words, ethico-political decisions configure the instituted meaning of the inscribed, which is another way of saying that undecidability confirms our claim about the contingent nature of objectivity.

So norms, whose generality makes them function as measures of equalization and therefore as indexes of equality, are worldly universals whose status is not that of an autonomous referent. Their claim to universality is subject to contestation and redescription, and therefore their status *as* universals is always undecidable and calls for an ethical involvement in 'political battles' or negotiations to assert their status and validity. The resulting measure, whatever it may be, is both a contingent outcome of the contest and a compromise among those who intervene in it. This compromise reflects the limits of any measure of universality by showing that impurity is not an accident but the essence of universality.

Ethico-political decisions and political battles concerning the universality of universals, however, do more too, since they introduce an element of force that was announced earlier and described in the example of women's quotas in political parties. Derrida raises this point theoretically when he maintains that force is not a secondary possibility that can be added – or not – as a supplement to the law, but rather an essential component of the very concept of justice as law (1992: 5).[10] Violence is intertwined with law in two ways: in its foundation and its conservation. The violence that institutes and positions law, what he calls 'law making violence', cannot rest on anything but itself (1992: 31). This is the case of revolutions, which Derrida discusses by invoking Benjamin's notion of the revolutionary general strike. While revolutionary violence provides the ground or foundation for legitimate power or justified authority, it is also a violence without a ground; a revolution is an original violence that inaugurates an order, so it cannot be justified or authorized by any anterior law or legitimacy (1992: 6, 14).[11] Violence is also present in the second sense of an authorized force directed to the preservation of existing laws. Derrida illustrates this with the English expression 'to enforce the law', for 'to enforce' presupposes the use of violence – in this case legitimate or authorized violence – in the conservation of law (1992: 5–7, 10–14, 31). People in democratic orders may dispute and condemn all norms, but these orders must also defend the norms that sustain democratic competition for power. These must be enforced – literally, secured through force – by either excluding or punishing those who go against them. That is why electoral laws often contain clauses that guarantee associational and ideological pluralism, but also stipulate limits to that pluralism in the case of groups whose charters contain non-democratic clauses or that endorse non-democratic means of action like armed struggle. He describes the police as a special hybrid or 'ignoble' case, in that it can publish ordinances (create binding norms) to uphold the legal order and therefore introduces ambiguity in the separation between founding and conservative violence. For Derrida the ambiguous condition of the police also reflects the paradox of iterability – a notion we flagged earlier – since it inscribes conservation in the essential structure of foundation; every institution is a promise that repeats itself through its alteration. Consequently, whether in its foundation or conservation, violence is lodged in the structure of legal norms. This violence reminds us that legal norms become measures of equality by overcoming a resistance and accepting an exclusion that compromises the purity of their universality.

More generally, any measure of universality arising in a democratic negotiation is bound to be limited or impure since some element of exclusion is built into it. That is the case, for example, with whatever stands for an index of toleration. There is little chance of thinking through the notion of toleration of otherness without some notion of the intolerable – that is, without some conception of the limits of toleration. While this limit is also open to polemic and dispute, the fact remains that pure or unbounded toleration is an empty claim. A similar limit is built into universal citizenship. Nineteenth-century liberalism introduced political equality through the notion of citizenship, yet citizenship was far from universal since women, illiterates and the young were excluded. It was challenged thereafter not because of the content of citizenship, but because of its dubious claim to universality. The very fact that it was formulated as universal made it a tactical device to contest exclusion and struggle to expand the scope of citizenship. In other words, it served to raise a polemic concerning its universality. Yet while the universality of citizenship functioned as a projected horizon for more egalitarian claims, it never assumed the status of absolute or pure universality. Some exclusion remained, whether due to minimum age requirements, place of birth or other reasons. At the same time, the institution of this impure universal citizenship erected a new stage for the formulation of egalitarian claims and the enactment of disputes concerning equality. It modified the field of polemics by redefining the space of commonality for the claims of particular groups. Following Rancière, and prefacing the point we will develop below, we may say that the argumentative plot that constructs universals also configures the perceptible space of argumentation: in a word, raises the question of commonality.

In the mean time it is worth flagging that the undecidability of the decision, justice as an event and the presence of force are indicative of the polemic status of universals in various ways. Firstly, it is pointless to expect that the conflictive relations between groups will dissolve itself in a Diaspora of reconciled autarkic differences, or give way to a single community based on an impossible fullness of universals – that is, pure or uncontaminated, 'universal' universals. The stabilization of the interplay between the exclusive and the inclusive modalities of the 'we' is governed by *différance*, and therefore is always a 'stabilization to come'. What is at stake in this 'to come' is the status of universals and of the space of commonality where the tension between the various types of 'we' is played out. Secondly, polemics concerning universality are caught in the gap between norms and their redescription; we are drawn continually into a political hermeneutics or war of interpretations concerning their status. This is another way of saying that involvement in a 'political battle' to verify the purchase of universals becomes not only desirable, but in fact inevitable. The status of universals arises in a political battle, and is therefore tied to hegemonic struggles where the space of contestation itself is configured in the course of the polemic concerning universals. Finally, the acceptance of a universal is not settled even after the juridico-political battles to sediment a figure for a universal are over. Here too, as in the case of undecidability concerning the decision of the judge, a spectre remains within the universal. This spectre of the undecidable haunts any sedimentation in a very direct way; it prevents any closure capable of 'settling' polemics in the sense of overcoming division and putting an end to grievances. In other words, it places whatever passes as the accepted measure of universality in the scene of repetition. Polemicization confirms and moves on this process of repetition.

4.5 Commonality Through Polemics

Now we should turn our attention to the question of commonality. Something we mentioned earlier about the essentialism of the elements may help introduce it. From a purely formal perspective it makes little difference if this essentialism derives from attempts to affirm an identity by excluding difference, or from efforts of minority groups to affirm their identity by hardening the frontiers between them. The underlying problem is the same: particularity is stressed at the expense of an apparent effacement of a space of commonality. The emphasis falls on the 'apparent' nature of this effacement. For example, while critics question the tendency of identity politics to promote a dangerous self-enclosure of particular groups, they admit that the bargaining position of women, blacks, gays and cultural minorities improved significantly since they began to speak up in defence of their interests (Steel 1992; Gitlin 1993; Hitchens 1993; Rorty 1990, 1992). The notion of 'bargaining position' only makes sense if there are at least two groups, if the groups engage in a negotiation, and if they expect to gain something from the negotiation – for example, a binding agreement concerning a disputed claim. Thus 'bargaining' refers to something wider than the group posing a claim, and consequently, it indicates that those engaged in a politics of identity are compelled to invoke something that transcends their pure particularity. The consequence of this is that in this scenario tokens of authority are no longer trumps. Agreement does not take place under authorized fiat. Instead, this has to be worked out. As no one needs reminding, with groups such as those mentioned above this is still in process, and perhaps to the extent that this is the case a democratic polity can be said to be taking place. This qualification prevents the reduction of democracy to the distribution of resources, if for no other reason than it recognizes that what a resource is always depends on its capacities at a particular moment in time. For example, access to education may have been won as a universal right enshrined in universal declarations. Yet if the nature of education is diluted in order to accommodate this injunction then its value is lessened. The measure of education itself becomes open to dispute, and consequently its purpose.

This alerts us to the effects of what is in fact an important theoretical and practical distinction concerning universality and particularity. At least two modalities of the 'we' are enacted in political bargaining. One is the 'we' that distinguishes a group from the wider political community in which it is immersed (us immigrants, us blacks and so on). The other is the 'we' that links the various groups as members of a wider political community (like us English or us democrats). This is not a distinction between a particular content and a universal category, but between fluctuating domains of exclusive and inclusive modalities of the 'we'. Guaraní, the language spoken by the Tupí Guaraní people of Brazil and Paraguay, has two different pronouns for this double inscription which distinguish a restricted 'we' (*oré*) from a more comprehensive we (*ñandé*). In democratic politics there is an enduring interplay between *oré* and *ñandé*, the exclusive and the inclusive 'we'. This interplay brings into focus the fact that the self-enclosure of groups is an impossible situation. This holds even where self-enclosure is imposed from outside, as under apartheid, or pursued from within by cultural minorities claiming that everyone should have their own exclusive domain. In both cases there is an explicit denial of a common space, but also an implicit acknowledgement of commonality, if only because of the resistance to exclusion or the pursuit of self-enclosure within a wider domain. More generally, as we saw in the example of quotas, where the *oré* of 'us women' engaged with other groups within the party *ñandé* of 'us socialists', exchanges among claimants, and the negotiation of some kind of measure for their conflicting claims, involves a tacit appeal to a space of commonality. Yet the paradox of this space, and of this measure, is that they are both a presupposition and an effect of polemic.

Let us look closer at this paradoxical commonality. In liberal democracies, inclusion in public space entails an initial political and juridical equality of participants as citizens and subjects of law and also their equality as individuals – what Lefort calls 'the recognition that human beings are made in one another's likeness' (Lefort 1988: 54). Even when fully realized and respected, which is seldom the case, these various modes of equalization do not cancel differences of class, gender and race, or the uneven distribution of cultural resources among participants, or their unequal access to positions of influence. The public realm is a 'space of commonality' that neither presupposes nor guarantees the full equality of people's share in it. There are fissures in the collective 'we' of any space of commonality. This is not only a feature of the liberal-democratic public sphere. It also characterizes the specialized publics of women, immigrants, gays, cultural minorities, and so on. A common space that is also a fissured space is not an oxymoron. It merely confirms the ontopolitical claim that unity arises from a division that cannot be fully eradicated and thus haunts any space of commonality from within. To state this differently, Rancière maintains that a political wrong might be addressed but cannot be righted. That is why he says that there can be equality, but not an egalitarian society. For the latter to exist, division would have to be overcome – that is, stabilization would have to be definitive and the distance between *oré* and *ñandé* would have to collapse. This is just another way of describing a reconciled society. Democratic processes bear witness to the impossibility of such reconciliation. They provide a setting for interminable disputes around countless grievances among non-reconcilable claimants. Perhaps that is why democracy could be defined as the political form that corroborates the fact of division, the ontopolitical status of the world as a divided world, and takes it on by working with and through that division.[12]

This 'fissured' commonality does not belittle the political import of public spaces. In fact it instigates political engagement. The pursuit of claims by the various *oré* involves a political task of filling the 'gap' between an actual state of affairs and a point 'x' that stands for the discursive construction of a desired state of affairs. This 'x' may stand for gender equality, as was the case in our example of quotas, but for many other things too. The set of political, juridical and 'human' modes of equalization turns public spaces into scenarios where a wrong can be made visible. Arendt makes visibility a crucial dimension of public space when she depicts it in Heideggerian terms as a *space of appearance*, where speech and action in concert become visible. The public realm comes into being 'whenever men are together in the manner of speech and action', for this creates 'a space between the participants which can find its proper location almost anytime and anywhere' (Arendt 1958: 198). A space of appearance is a space of visibility in the usual sense of opposition to secrecy or concealment, and perhaps in Arendt's sense of a quasi-aristocratic space for agonistic contests among citizens who strive for recognition through great speeches and deeds. There is more to it, however, especially with the advent of modernity and its assertion of the contingency of order. Marx and Engels saw this clearly. In an often-quoted passage of the *Manifesto* they claimed that with modernity, which they often conflated with capitalism, 'All that is solid melts into air, all that is holy is profaned.' In this melting and profanation contingency designates the metastable nature of order, its existence as a continual process of institution and reinstitution. More to the point, for us the contingency of order refers to the contestable and therefore polemic status of objectivity. The reference to objectivity adds a twist to the idea of visibility by linking it with the enunciation of that which has not been publicly discussed, with the standing of a sedimented enunciation, and more importantly, with putting in question the limits of that which can be enunciated. Thus public space as a space of appearance turns out to be more pedestrian and less heroic than Arendt wished, but also more political, since it becomes a space where themes, grievances and identities come to life and irrupt in the public conscience. We could say, paraphrasing Lefort's observations about the political, that this sense of visibility makes public space a scenario for shaping (*mise en forme*) grievances concerning a wrong, which implies both giving a meaning to (*mise en sens*) and staging those grievances (*mise en scène*) (Lefort 1988: 216–20).

This activity of shaping, staging and giving sense does not reduce visibility to a mere disclosure of grievances. There is no disclosure without a concomitant disputation to make disclosure effective and to pursue a claim. This is the creative aspect of contestation. Public space is a space of disputes where class, gender, race or other groups can emerge and engage in democratic struggles aiming to address the perceived wrong – that is, to bridge the gap between the existing and the desired state of affairs through contingent political crossings. They are contingent in the double sense that the conception of the objective, the type of 'bridge' and the way of achieving the crossing could have always been different, and that no crossing settles once and for all the grievance that sparked the dispute. Both senses refer to the contestable status of objectivity and to the fact that reconciliation is not necessary for commonality since a community effect is produced through polemics itself. Moreover, we should notice that while these crossings revolve around the specific issue at stake – the wrong in question – they also have an effect on the standing and the identity of the parties involved, and on the very configuration of the field where their engagement is enacted. Whenever there is polemic there is public space, so public space is not only or not merely the site where politics is said legitimately to take place. It is what occurs whenever there is contestation. In fact, the belief that a public space cannot occur until a practice of legitimation is established represents a loss of nerve on the part of modern political thought, but also a disavowal as proponents of such views always speak from a situation in which legitimation is in crisis, to reactivate an old problematic. Public space is a space of dispute, but the event of dispute also creates public space and modifies what that space was previously thought to encompass. For example, the dispute concerning the universality of citizenship sought to recast its universality through the inclusion of workers, women and the young; but it did more too, since it transformed the modes of political identification, the form of engagement and the field of struggle by positioning the various groups within the settings of the political system without putting an end to divisions among those included in the domain of citizens. Hence the resources of politics were themselves transformed, for good or ill.

Rancière explains the creation and transformation of the space of polemic engagement as follows (Rancière 1995a, 1995b). He claims that for politics to exist there must be named subjects. Here we can extend the earlier discussion of subjectivity. It is the existence of subjects of enunciation that make it possible to say 'we' workers, women, patriots or what have you. These various 'we' – in the sense of *oré* – create apparatuses of subjectivation where a subject is named to expose a wrong and create a community around a particular dispute that makes evident a non-community. There is a 'non-community' because the grievances that give rise to subjects of enunciation unite and separate interlocutors in a dispute. One can see this in disputes concerning universal citizenship as a measure of political equality or in the pursuit of quotas as a means to fulfil gender equality within a political party. In both cases there is a 'coming together' of the participants under the aegis of a dispute that also splits them into two (or more) camps. In this sense the *oré* or exclusive 'we' are symptoms of what Rancière calls an absent community, of the fact that community is not realized, does not exist already but is in the making, as it were – what Derrida describes as the *à-venir* of community or community 'to come'. Taking up Butler's analysis, this can be extended to the very name of the community under which subjection occurs. So the paradox involved in polemics concerning universality is that there is (or could be) a community in so far as it is continually contested. One must stage a polemical *topos* to handle the wrong and demonstrate – as in the examples of citizenship and gender equality – one's right to be included. This demonstration is *tropic*. Political argumentation must polemically construct the scene of its validity, which is in fact the space of commonality for handling a wrong. That is why Rancière concludes that one cannot claim that there is *either* community or nothing at all, but rather what he calls 'the politics of the in-between'; we are always caught in between names, cultures and identities, challenging the existing space of commonality and reinstituting it at the same time.

So, generally speaking, putting universals like 'equality' to the test is actually a means to negotiate their status, and the struggles waged by the various *oré* reveal that a certain commonality comes into play even if it is to dispute its validity. Drawing from this we could say that Rancière's politics of the in-between actually names the interval whereby politics is possible. Politics manifests itself through the constitution of subjects of enunciation and the enactment of polemics between them, and this generates a community effect through the contestation of whatever stands for community. Put differently, the staging of a polemic within the double inscription of the *oré* and the *ñandé* both presupposes and configures a space of commonality which cannot coincide with itself. There are always many, and this manifold does not necessarily coincide with the same. This bears witness to the structural necessity of division. The corollary is that the identity of both the parties and the terrain of struggle or ground of polemic – the space of commonality – is shaped by that dispute too. This means that equality and difference can be maintained without the presumption of totality that determines their relation: that is to say, commonality occurs without relying on a referent external to it as determination or internal to it as a logic of immanence.

Notes

1. Here we differ considerably from W. B. Gallie's thesis of the 'essentially contested' nature of concepts, although not from the description that supports it.
2. As Derrida (1994a: 41) says, 'Unification and legitimacy never establish themselves successfully except by making people forget that there never was any natural unity or prior foundation.' In a similar vein, Slavoj Žižek (1994: 204) maintains that hegemony is exerted when the violent irruption of an element is perceived as 'a matter of course': that is to say, '"hegemony" designates usurping violence whose violent character is sublated.'
3. Mike Shapiro (1999) has suggested a possible ethical approach to the relation between the same and its contingency. Here the emphasis is on the singularity of the relation.
4. 'A wrong results from the fact that the rules of the genre of discourse by which one judges are not those of the judged genre of discourse' (Lyotard 1988: xi, also 5, 8–11).
5. We can only refer here to the more familiar culturalist analysis of this scenario – for example, in the work of Jameson and Baudrillard. We would not disagree with the general point both authors share: namely, that value is determined culturally, which means that the domain of culture expands to include money. One must not underestimate the role that 'national cultures' play in this. Culture is increasingly the referent that guarantees national value.

6. In fact, he says, politics consists of leading the community through discord itself, through the impossibility of the people being equal to themselves. We saw how this idea of order worked in the case of a 'fissured commonality' when we discussed the formation of a space of commonality through polemics.

7. To put it slightly differently, this means that the ontopolitical condition of division also affects the standing of the contestants. This was already pointed out in the discussion about commonality. The unity of the claimants does not remain untouched by the conflicts into which they enter, for antagonistic relations both configure and reconfigure the identity of the intervening parties.

8. For an intervention within this aporetic space which directs it towards the question of technology and time, see Beardsworth (1996).

9. Here is where one perceives the limits of the Schmittian enterprise. In his case the decision, by the very fact that it is believed to have been taken, and by the fact that it is believed that it is possible to take it, at the same time and immediately, occupies and exhausts the position of its enunciation. As we mentioned earlier, Schmitt usually refers to this as the State, or sovereignty, but as there is no necessary relation between the content of the enunciation and the act through which it is enunciated, Schmitt simply randomizes the State (or other sovereign institution) across a space which he insisted must be closed, but which can only be closed in so far as a decision is taken to close through the institution of a frontier. Such a performative can never get off the ground, although it may unify by virtue of its spectacular experience. Rather, because such an act presupposes the interruption of time, the time of decision, it cannot be said to be complete. The consequences of this are clearly laid out in Beardsworth (1996). Similarly, it is not enunciated directly but through the temporal dislocation of deliberation.

10. See also Žižek's discussion of Derrida's position in relation to Lacanian approaches to the question of political violence in Žižek (1994: 204–5 and 216–17).

11. Schmitt (1985: 12–13) develops a similar argument for the relation between decision and legal norms in an exceptional situation.

12. The idea of 'ontopolitical' interpretation comes from Connolly (1995: 1–40), who uses it to acknowledge the weight of ontological claims in political and theoretical arguments, but also to undermine the more restrictive and totalizing connotations of the

term 'ontology'. The reference to the constitutive status of division – a basic tenet of modernity – is an ontopolitical claim in our argument. The Hobbesian absolutist response to such division is to conceive political order as a mode of overcoming or suppressing conflict, and therefore antagonistic relations, whereas the democratic solution both acknowledges the ineradicable nature of conflict and incorporates it in a regulated way. Lefort (1988: 18) takes up this point when he discusses the relation between political conflict and the unity of society in a democracy:

> The erection of a political stage on which competition can take place shows that division is, in a general way, constitutive of the very unity of society. Or to put it another way, the legitimation of purely political conflict contains within it the principle of legitimation of social conflict in all its forms.

Bibliography

Agamben, Giorgio (1993), *The Coming Community*, Minnesota: University of Minnesota Press

Appadurai, Arjun (1992), 'Disjuncture and Difference in the Global Cultural Economy', in Bruce Robbins (ed.), *The Phantom Public Sphere*, Minneapolis: University of Minnesota Press, pp. 269–96

Arendt, Hannah (1958), *The Human Condition*, Chicago: University of Chicago Press

Arendt, Hannah (1982), *Lectures on Kant's Political Philosophy*, Brighton: Harvester

Balibar, Etienne (1991), 'Citizen Subject', in Eduardo Cadava et. al (eds), *Who Comes After the Subject?*, London and New York: Routledge, pp. 33–57

Balibar, Etienne (1994), 'Subject and Subjectivation', in Joan Copjec (ed.), *Supposing the Subject*, London: Verso, pp. 1–15

Balibar, Etienne (1995), 'Ambiguous Universality', *Differences*, Vol. 7, No. 1, pp. 48–74

Baudrillard, Jean (1997), *Art and Artefact*, London and New York: Routledge

Bauman, Zygmunt (1989), 'Modernity and Ambivalence', *Theory, Culture and Society*, Vol. 7, No. 3, pp. 141–69

Beardsworth, Richard (1996), *Derrida and the Political*, London and New York: Routledge

Beiner, Ronald and William James Booth (1993), *Kant and Political Philosophy: The Contemporary Legacy*, New Haven and London: Yale University Press

Bellamy, Elizabeth J. (1993), 'Discourses of Impossibility: Can Psychoanalysis be Political?', *Diacritics*, Vol. 23, No. 1, pp. 24–38

Berlant, Lauren (1997), *The Queen of America Goes to Washington City: Essays on Sex and Citizenship*, Durham and London: Duke University Press

Blumenberg, Hans (1983), *The Legitimacy of the Modern Age*, Cambridge, Mass: MIT Press

Bobbio, Norberto (1989), *Democracy and Dictatorship: The Nature and Limits of State Power*, Cambridge: Polity Press

Brittan, Samuel (1988), *A Restatement of Economic Liberalism*, Basingstoke and London: Macmillan

Butler, Judith (1993), 'Poststructuralism and Postmarxism', *Diacritics*, Vol. 23, No. 4, pp. 3–11

Butler, Judith (1997a), *Excitable Speech: A Politics of the Performative*, London and New York: Routledge

Butler, Judith (1997b), *The Psychic Life of Power: Theories in Subjection*, Stanford: Stanford University Press

Connolly, William (1991), *Identity/Difference: Democratic Negotiations of Political Paradox*, Ithaca and London: Cornell University Press

Connolly, William (1995), *The Ethos of Pluralization*, Minnesota: University of Minnesota Press

Coole, Diana (1998), 'The Politics of Reading Nietzsche', *Political Studies*, Vol. 46, No. 2, pp. 348–63

Copjec, Joan (1994), *Read My Desire: Lacan Against the Historicists*, Cambridge, Mass: MIT Press

Cornell, Drucilla (1995), 'Rethinking the Beyond of the Real', *Cardozo Law Review*, Vol. 16, pp. 729–92

Critchley, Simon (1997), *Very Little . . . Almost Nothing*, London and New York: Routledge

Dallmayr, Fred (1993), *The Other Heidegger*, Ithaca: Cornell University Press

Davidson, Donald (1984), *Inquiries into Truth and Interpretation*, Oxford: Clarendon Press

de Certeau, Michel (1984), *The Practice of Everyday Life*, Berkeley: University of California Press

Deleuze, Gilles and Felix Guattari (1994), *What is Philosophy?*, London: Verso

Derrida, Jacques (1981), 'Economimesis', *Diacritics*, Vol. 11, No. 2, pp. 3–25

Derrida, Jacques (1988), 'Signature Event Context' (1971), in *Limited Inc.*, Evanston, Illinois: Northwestern University Press, pp. 1–23

Derrida, Jacques (1992), 'Force of Law: The "Mystical Foundation of Authority"', in Drucilla Cornell et al. (eds), *Deconstruction and the Possibility of Justice*, London and New York: Routledge, pp. 3–67

Derrida, Jacques (1994a), 'The Deconstruction of Actuality', interview in *Radical Philosophy*, No. 68, Autumn, pp. 28–41

Derrida, Jacques (1994b), 'Nietzsche and the Machine', interview with Richard Beardsworth, *Journal of Nietzsche Studies*, No. 7, pp. 7–66

Derrida, Jacques (1995), *Specters of Marx*, London and New York: Routledge

Derrida, Jacques (1996), 'Remarks on Deconstruction and Pragmatism', in

Chantal Mouffe (ed.), *Deconstruction and Pragmatism*, London and New York: Routledge, pp. 76–87

Derrida, Jacques (1997), *Politics of Friendship*, London: Verso

Descombes, Vincent (1997), 'Nietzsche's French Moment', in Ferry and Renault, pp. 70–91

Diskin, Jonathan (1994), 'New Reflections on the Revolution of Our Time', *Rethinking Marxism*, Vol. 7, No. 1, pp. 138–44

Dolar, Mladen (1995), 'The Legacy of the Enlightenment: Foucault and Lacan', in Erica Carter et al. (eds), *Cultural Remix: Theories of Politics and the Popular*, London: Lawrence and Wishart, pp. 261–78

Düttman, Alexander Garcia (1996), *At Odds with Aids: Thinking and Talking about a Virus*, Stanford: Stanford University Press

Düttman, Alexander Garcia (1997), 'The Culture of Polemic: Misrecognizing Recognition', *Radical Philosophy*, Vol. 81, pp. 27–34

Ferry, Luc (1990), 'La cuestión del sujeto en la filosofía contemporánea', in various authors, *El sujeto europeo*, Madrid: Fundación Pablo Iglesias, pp. 61–76

Ferry, Luc and Alain Renaut (eds), (1997) *Why we are Not Nietzscheans*, Chicago: University of Chicago Press

Foster, Hal (1996), *The Return of the Real*, Cambridge, Mass: MIT Press

Foucault, Michel (1978), *The History of Sexuality* Vol. 1 London: Penguin

Foucault, Michel (1982), 'The Subject and Power', in Hubert L. Dreyfus and Paul Rabinow, *Michel Foucault: Beyond Structuralism and Hermeneutics*, Brighton: Harvester Wheatsheaf, pp. 208–26

Foucault, Michel (1984a), 'Polemics, Politics and Problematizations', in Paul Rabinow (ed.) *The Foucault Reader*, London: Penguin, pp. 381–90

Foucault, Michel (1984b), 'What is Enlightenment?', in Paul Rabinow (ed.) *The Foucault Reader*, London: Penguin, pp. 32–50

Foucault, Michel (1993), 'Kant on Enlightenment and Revolution', in Mike Gane and Terry Johnson (eds), *Foucault's New Domains*, London and New York: Routledge, pp. 10–18

Fraser, Nancy (1992), 'Rethinking the Public Sphere', in Craig Calhoun (ed.), *Habermas and the Public Sphere*, Cambridge, Mass: MIT Press, pp. 109–42

Freud, Sigmund (1984), 'On Narcissism: An Introduction', in *On Metapsychology: The Theory of Psychoanalysis*, Pelican Freud Library, Vol. 11, Harmondsworth: Penguin, pp. 59–98

Frye, Charles E. (1966), 'Carl Schmitt's Concept of the Political', *Journal of Politics*, Vol. XXVIII, No. 4

Fuss, Diana (1989), *Essentially Speaking: Feminism, Nature and Difference*, London and New York: Routledge

Fuss, Diana (1995), *Identity Papers*, London and New York: Routledge

Genette, Gérard (1982), *Figures of Literary Discourse*, Oxford: Basil Blackwell

Gitlin, Todd (1993), 'The Rise of "Identity Politics"', *Dissent*, Vol. 40, No. 2, Spring, pp. 172–77

Goux, Jean Joseph (1990), *Symbolic Economies: After Marx and Freud*, Ithaca: Cornell University Press

Griggers, Camilla (1997), *Becoming-Woman*, Minneapolis: University of Minnesota Press

Guha, Ranajit and Gayatri Chakravorty Spivak (eds) (1989), *Selected Subaltern Studies*, New York: Oxford University Press

Hacking, Ian (1975), *The Emergence of Probability*, Cambridge: Cambridge University Press

Hampton, Jean (1989), 'Should Political Philosophy be Done without Metaphysics?', *Ethics*, Vol. 99, pp. 791–814

Hardt, Michael and Antonio Negri (1994), *Labor of Dionysus: A Critique of the State Form*, Minneapolis: University of Minnesota Press

Hart, Kevin (1989), *Trespass of the Sign: Deconstruction, Theology and Philosophy*, Cambridge: Cambridge University Press

Heller, Agnes (1990), *Can Modernity Survive?*, Cambridge: Polity Press

Hitchens, Christopher (1993), 'The New Complainers', *Dissent*, Vol. 40, No. 4, Fall, pp. 560–64

Honig, Bonnie (1993), *Political Theory and the Displacement of Politics*, Ithaca: Cornell University Press

Howard, Dick (1977), *The Marxian Legacy*, Basingstoke and London: Macmillan

Howard, Dick (1989), *Defining the Political*, Basingstoke and London: Macmillan

Kant, Immanuel (1929), *The Critique of Pure Reason*, Basingstoke and London: Macmillan

Kant, Immanuel (1989), *The Moral Law: Groundwork of the Metaphysic of Morals*, London and New York: Routledge

Kant, Immanuel (1991a), 'An Answer to the Question: "What is Enlightenment?"', in Hans Reiss (ed.), *Kant: Political Writings*, Cambridge University Press, pp. 54–60

Kant, Immanuel (1991b), 'Idea for a Universal History with a Cosmopolitan Purpose', in Hans Reiss (ed.), *Kant: Political Writings*, Cambridge University Press, pp. 41–53

Kantorowicz, Ernst (1957), *The King's Two Bodies*, Princeton: Princeton University Press

Kelly, George Armstrong (1969), *Idealism, Politics and History: Sources of Hegelian Thought*, London: Cambridge University Press

Kolb, David (1986), *The Critique of Pure Modernity: Hegel, Heidegger and After*, Chicago: University of Chicago Press

Kristeva, Julia (1975), 'The System and the Speaking Subject', in Thomas A. Sebeok (ed.), *The Tell Tale Sign: A Survey of Semiotics*, Lisse, Netherlands: Peter de Ridder Press, pp. 47–55

Kristeva, Julia (1998), 'The Subject in Process', in Patrick ffrench and Roland-François Lack (eds), *The Tel Quel Reader*, London and New York: Routledge

Lacan, Jacques (1998), *The Seminar of Jacques Lacan Book 1: Freud's Papers on Technique 1953–54*, Jacques-Alain Miller (ed.), Cambridge: Cambridge University Press

Laclau, Ernesto (1990), *New Reflections on the Revolution of Our Times*, London: Verso

Laclau, Ernesto (1991), 'Community and its Paradoxes: Richard Rorty's "Liberal Utopia"', in Miami Theory Collective (ed.), *Community at Loose Ends*, Minnesota: Minnesota University Press, pp. 83–98

Laclau, Ernesto (1992), 'Universalism, Particularism and the Question of Identity', *October*, No. 61, Summer, pp. 83–90

Laclau, Ernesto (1994), 'Why do Empty Signifiers Matter to Politics?' in Jeffrey Weeks (ed.), *The Lesser Evil and the Greater Good*, London: Rivers Oram, pp. 167–78

Laclau, Ernesto and Chantal Mouffe (1985), *Hegemony and Socialist Strategy*, London: Verso

Laclau, Ernesto and Lilian Zac (1994), 'Minding the Gap', in Ernesto Laclau (ed.), *The Making of Political Identities*, London: Verso

Landry, Donna and Gerald Maclean (1991), 'Re-Reading Laclau and Mouffe', *Rethinking Marxism*, Vol. 4, No. 4, pp. 41–60

Larmore, Charles (1996), *The Morals of Modernity*, Cambridge: Cambridge University Press

Lash, Scott and John Urry (1987), *The End of Organized Capitalism*, Cambridge: Polity Press

Laursen, John Christian (1986), 'The Subversive Kant: The Vocabulary of "Public" and "Publicity"', *Political Theory*, Vol. 14, No. 4, pp. 584–603

Lefort, Claude (1986), *The Political Forms of Modern Society*, Cambridge: Polity Press

Lefort, Claude (1988), *Democracy and Political Theory*, Cambridge: Polity Press

Lefort, Claude (1990), 'Renaissance of Democracy', *Praxis International*, Vol. 10, Nos 1 and 2, April and July, pp. 1–13

Leyshon, Andrew and Nigel Thrift (1997), *MoneySpace: Geographies of Monetary Transformation*, London and New York: Routledge

Locke, John (1991), *Two Treatises on Government*, Cambridge: Cambridge University Press

Lyotard, Jean-François (1988), *The Differend*, Manchester: Manchester University Press.

Manin, Bernard (1987), 'On Legitimacy and Political Deliberation', *Political Theory*, Vol. 15, No. 3, August, pp. 338–68

Mbembe, Achille and Janet Roitman (1995), 'Figures of the Subject in Times of Crisis', *Public Culture*, Vol. 7, No. 2, pp. 323–52

Mouffe, Chantal (1993), *The Return of the Political*, London: Verso

Mouffe, Chantal (1995), 'Democracy and Pluralism: A Critique of the Rationalist Approach', *Cardozo Law Review*, Vol. 16, pp. 1533–45

Mulhall, Stephen and Adam Swift (1992), *Liberals and Communitarians*, Oxford: Basil Blackwell

Nancy, Jean-Luc (1997), 'The Insufficiency of "Values" and the Necessity of "Sense"', *Cultural Values*, Vol. 1, No. 1, April, pp. 127–31

Nietzsche, Friedrich (1911), 'On Truth and Falsity in Their Ultramoral Sense', in Oscar Levy (ed.), *The Complete Works of Friedrich Nietzsche, Vol. II, Edinburgh: Darien pp. 173–92

Offe, Claus (1985), *Disorganized Capitalism*, Cambridge, Mass: MIT Press

O'Neill, Onora (1986), 'The Public Use of Reason', *Political Theory*, Vol. 14, No. 4, pp. 523–51

Perelman, Chaim (1971), 'The New Rhetoric', in Yehoshua Bar-Hillel (ed.), *Pragmatics of Natural Languages*, Dordrecht, Holland: D. Reidel, pp. 145–9

Perelman, Chaim and Lucie Ollbrechts-Tyteca (1969), trans. By John Wilkinson and Purcell Weaver, *The New Rhetoric: A Treatise on Argumentation*, Notre Dame, Indiana: University of Notre Dame Press

Pippin, Robert B. (1991), *Modernism as a Philosophical Problem: On the Dissatisfactions of European High Culture*, Oxford: Basil Blackwell

Pippin, Robert B. (1997), *Idealism as Modernism*, Cambridge: Cambridge University Press

Rancière, Jacques (1995a), 'Post-democracy, Politics and Philosophy', interview in *Angelaki*, Vol. 1, No. 3, pp. 171–8

Rancière, Jacques (1995b), 'Politics, Identification and Subjectivization', in John Rajchman (ed.), *The Identity in Question*, London and New York: Routledge, pp. 63–72

Rancière, Jacques (1995c), *On the Shores of Politics*, London: Verso

Rancière, Jacques (1998), *Disagreement: Politics and Philosophy*, Minneapolis: University of Minnesota Press

Rawls, John (1971), *A Theory of Justice*, Oxford: Oxford University Press

Rawls, John (1980), 'Kantian Constructivism in Moral Theory', *Journal of Philosophy*, Vol. LXXVII, No. 9, pp. 515–72

Rawls, John (1985) 'Justice as Fairness: Political Not Metaphysical', *Philosophy and Public Affairs*, Vol. 14, No. 3, pp. 223–51

Rawls, John (1993), 'Themes in Kant's Moral Philosophy', in Ronald Beiner and William James Booth (eds), *Kant and Political Philosophy: The Contemporary Legacy*, New Haven and London: Yale University Press, pp. 291–319

Rawls, John (1995), 'Reply To Habermas', *Journal of Philosophy*, Vol. XCII, No. 3, pp. 132–80

Ricœur, Paul (1988), 'Le Cercle de la démonstration', *Esprit*, No. 2, pp. 78–88

Ricœur, Paul (1990), 'John Rawls: De l'autonomie morale à la fiction du contrat social', *Revue de Métaphysique et de Morale*, No. 3, pp. 367–84

Rorty, Richard (1990), 'Two Cheers for the Cultural Left', *South Atlantic Quarterly*, Vol. 89, No. 1, Winter, pp. 227–34

Rorty, Richard (1992), 'On Intellectuals in Politics', *Dissent*, Vol. 39, No. 2, Spring, pp. 265–7

Rosen, Stanley (1987), *Hermeneutics as Politics*, Oxford: Odéon/Oxford University Press

Sandel, Michael (1982), *Liberalism and the Limits of Justice*, Cambridge: Cambridge University Press

Schmitt, Carl (1985), *Political Theology: Four Chapters on the Concept of Sovereignty* (1922, 1934), Cambridge, Mass: MIT Press

Schmitt, Carl (1996), *The Concept of the Political* (1932), translation and introduction by George Schwab and a foreword by Tracy Strong, Chicago: University of Chicago Press

Schürmann, Reiner (1986) 'On Constituting Oneself an Anarchistic Subject', *Praxis International*, Vol. 6, pp. 294–310

Schürmann, Reiner (1987), *Heidegger on Being and Acting: From Principles to Anarchy*, Bloomington: Indiana University Press

Shapiro, Michael J. (1993), *Reading 'Adam Smith': Desire, History and Value*, London: Sage

Shapiro, Michael J. (1999), *Cinematic Political Thought*, Edinburgh and New York: Edinburgh University Press and New York University Press

Skinner, Quentin (1996), *Reason and Rhetoric in the Philosophy of Hobbes*, Cambridge: Cambridge University Press

Smith, Anna-Marie (1998), *Laclau and Mouffe: The Radical Democratic Imaginary*, London and New York: Routledge

Staten, Henry (1984), *Wittgenstein and Derrida*, Lincoln and London: University of Nebraska Press

Steel, Shelby (1992), 'The New Sovereignty', *Harper's Magazine*, July, pp. 49–53

Taylor, Charles (1989), 'Cross-Purposes: The Liberal-Communitarian Debate', in Nancy L. Rosenblum (ed.), *Liberalism and the Moral Life*, Cambridge, Mass: Harvard University Press

Thompson, John B. (1984), *Studies in the Theory of Ideology*, Cambridge: Polity Press

Vattimo, Gianni (1992), *The Transparent Society*, Cambridge: Polity Press

Venn, Couze (1997), 'Beyond Enlightenment: After the Subject of Foucault, Who Comes?', *Theory, Culture and Society*, Vol. 14, No. 3, 1–28

Visker, Rudi (1993), 'Transcultural Vibrations', mimeo, Catholic University of Leuven

Weber, Samuel (1992), 'Taking Exception To Decision: Walter Benjamin and Carl Schmitt', *Diacritics*, Vol. 22, No. 3, pp. 5–18

Wittgenstein, Ludwig (1983), *Philosophical Investigations*, Oxford: Basil Blackwell

Woodward, Bob (1995), *The Agenda*, book reviewed in *The Independent on Sunday*, London, 12 February

Yack, Bernard (1993), 'The Problem With Kantian Liberalism', in Beiner and Booth, pp. 224–44

Young, Iris Marion (1989), 'Polity and Group Difference: A Critique of the Ideal of Universal Citizenship', *Ethics*, Vol. 99, pp. 250–74

Žižek, Slavoj (1988), *The Sublime Object of Ideology*, London: Verso

Žižek, Slavoj (1990), 'Beyond Discourse Analysis', in Laclau (1990), pp. 249–60

Žižek, Slavoj (1991), *For They Know What They Do*, London: Verso

Žižek, Slavoj (1994), *The Metastases of Enjoyment*, London: Verso

Žižek, Slavoj (1997), 'Multiculturalism, Or, the Cultural Logic of Multi-national Capitalism', *New Left Review*, No. 225, pp. 28–52

Index

www.ingramcontent.com/pod-product-compliance
Lightning Source LLC
Chambersburg PA
CBHW032144020426
42334CB00016B/1224